Praise for
It's Your Life, Live BIG!

"I am fond of this saying, 'Most people aim at nothing in life and hit it with amazing accuracy.' Josh's book helps you clearly identify your personal definition of success and shows you how to achieve it with amazing accuracy."

Dr. Tony Alessandra
Hall-of-Fame Keynote Speaker and author of 27 books
including *The Platinum Rule*

"Josh Hinds is someone who has overcome huge obstacles to live big in his life and in his book, *It's Your Life, Live BIG!* he teaches proven principles that will help you to live big in your life as well."

Ty Bennett
Author of *The Power of Influence*

"Josh proves that with a strong enough desire and a road map to get there, anyone can achieve their goals and realize their dreams. Fortunately, in this terrific book, he provides us with the information we need in order to do just that. As always, Josh holds nothing back; he shares it all - including the difficulties he faced and overcame along the way. From thinking the right way...to the 'workarounds' that can help you achieve the improbable, follow Josh's sage wisdom and advice and you'll find yourself living a rich, successful life. And, you'll Live BIG!"

Bob Burg
Co-author of *The Go-Giver*
and author of *The Art of Persuasion*

"Josh Hinds is a master at motivating people to achieve their best. In his work, *It's Your Life, Live BIG!* he lays out not only the motivation which we all need to get and keep moving, but he gives you the specific tools. I loved what he said about keeping it simple. Too often we complicate what is needed.

Josh takes you by the hand in this powerful book so that you can achieve your goals. Josh relates his real-life challenges he has faced. This guy lives in the real world! And the best part of that is that he is there with you encouraging you, offering specific advice and help showing you what to do to conquer your challenges.

This is a book you'll want to get not only for yourself but for those around you who need both motivation and the specific steps to take to achieve your goals. If it is your sales that need boosting, this is a great book to read. If it is your personal life that needs boosting, this book will inspire and motivate you. If it is the area of relationships where you need a little extra coaching, Josh will help you with this as well. *It's Your Life, Live BIG!* is a book you'll want to not just read, but devour. I loved it when I read it and I know you will also."

Terry L. Brock, MBA, CSP, CPAE
Member, Professional Speaker Hall of Fame
Certified Speaking Professional
Editor in Chief, AT&T Networking Exchange Blog

"Life is amazing! Josh reminds us how to LIVE BIG and make the most out of our experiences in life! His book will motivate and challenge you in ways never seen before!"

Brad Cohen
Author of book and
Hallmark Hall of Fame movie,
Front of the Class

"*It's Your Life, Live BIG* is a book in which everyone can appreciate the valuable sagaciousness that Josh Hinds shares with his readers. Josh's perspicacious way of simplifying life's lessons into obtainable goals leaves you feeling confident and not overwhelmed. Josh shows you the possibilities in life instead of the improbabilities, that you too can live the life you dream of. Who wants to live a small life when you can live a BIG life? As Josh says, *It's Your Life, Live BIG!*"

Michelle Colon-Johnson
Motivational Speaker, Life Coach

"*It's Your Life, Live BIG!* is exactly the can't-put-it-down book I'd expect from Josh Hinds. He has an indomitable spirit that comes through on every page and inspires and empowers you to take the action you most need to 'LIVE BIG.' He provides not just the motivation but the real time tools, strategies, and core actions you must implement to ignite your full potential and play full out instead of just sitting on the sidelines of life. Josh has done this and continues to every day in every way. Don't miss this!"

Melissa Galt
Author of *Celebrate Your Life:*
The Art of Celebrating Everyday

"To say Josh Hinds is a great motivator is a vast understatement. Using his poignant life story as a jumping-off point, Josh paints a vivid picture of triumphing over adversity and guiding others to do the same. If you want to be inspired to tackle just about any work or life challenge, read *It's Your Life, Live BIG!*"

Libby Gill
Business Coach and
Bestselling Author of *YOU UNSTUCK*

"Josh Hinds can speak with authority about adversity, he chooses instead to speak about the success lessons and principles that have given him the power to overcome it. In *Live BIG*, Josh turns his impassioned message of possibility and empowerment into a series of lessons and actionable "do its" that apply universally to overcoming any challenge and achieving any goal we may set for ourselves. His Southern Gentleman wit and inclusive language makes us feel hugged and honored rather than admonished or exhorted. A delightful read, full of wise insights and proven success principles."

Dixie "Dynamite" Gillespie
Entrepreneur Coach, dixiedynamitecoaching.com

"To Live Big you must think Big. Read this great book and let Josh Hinds inspire you to be your best."

Jon Gordon
Best-selling author of
The Energy Bus and The Seed

"One of the very first relationships I had in the personal development world and on the internet was with Josh Hinds. He recognized early on what a great tool the web could be for helping people grow and he's always been a leader in providing outstanding content for his readers. *It's Your Life, Live BIG!* is another example of that, but in this case we also get the added inspiration and lessons from Josh's own personal struggles to LIVE BIG! And LIVE BIG he has by overcoming what many would see as an overwhelming obstacle on his way to becoming a noted and successful speaker and coach. Outstanding reading!"

Vic Johnson
Founder, AsAManThinketh.net

"Josh Hinds is a man on a mission who inspires people with his actions, as well as with his words. I recommend you read this book and then re-read it, and share it with people in your network. It will inspire and empower all who pick it up!"

Willie Jolley
Best Selling Author of
A Setback Is A Setup For A Comeback
and *An Attitude of Excellence*

"Josh Hinds is a phenomenal human being who has overcome life's obstacles and succeeded by doing the right things in life. Live BIG is a roadmap to reaching your goals in life from someone who was selling mortgages at 15, dealt brilliantly with a huge challenge at 18, and created a BIG business! Get *Live BIG* and Live BIG!"

Howard Partridge
Author of *7 Secrets of a Phenomenal L.I.F.E.*

"Josh's new book, *It's Your Life, Live Big!* gives you the lessons and the tools necessary to make the best choices for living your best life. In each of the 17 chapters Josh shares insights, applications and action steps to keep you motivated and moving forward. This is an excellent book for those looking to get unstuck and plan a successful life!"

Michelle Prince
Best-Selling Author of *Winning in Life Now*
Zig Ziglar Motivational Speaker

"Josh Hinds had plenty of excuses to shrink into defeat and mediocrity, but chose to face his challenges with big dreams and big actions! *Live BIG!* is a must-read book for anyone who wants to overcome their obstacles and live the life they were created for!"

Thom Scott
CIFP (Chief Instigator of Fun and Profits),
Intentional Entrepreneur & Legacy Architect,
MBA, CeMM

"Josh has overcome some extraordinary challenges to live his best life. This book shares his story. And inspires you to change the game."

Robin Sharma
#1 bestselling author of
The Leader Who Had No Title

It's Your Life

LIVE
BIG

It's Your Life LIVE BIG

Josh Hinds

sound wisdom
Shippensburg, PA

Sound Wisdom
167 Walnut Bottom Road
Shippensburg, PA 17257

www.soundwisdom.com

This book and all other Sound Wisdom books are available at bookstores and distributors worldwide.

ISBN 13: 978-1-937879-02-0
ISBN Ebook: 978-1-937879-05-1

For Worldwide Distribution, Printed in the U.S.A.

3 4 5 6 7 / 16 15 14 13 12

Contents

ACKNOWLEDGEMENTS

Rather than even attempt to thank everyone individually who deserves my acknowledgement and run the risk of missing someone, I will instead mention just a few people by name, with the full understanding that if you have ever been, or are a part of my life, personally or professionally, then you too are deserving of my acknowledgement, thanks and appreciation. The ideas shared in this book would not be possible without my life experiences. You my friend are an invaluable part of that.

First, I would like to thank the good LORD above for every blessing, as well as challenge, which has come into my life. It is through not only the good times, but life's challenges that I have learned to "LIVE BIG" and in doing so, hope that what I will be sharing with you in the book will help you to do so as well.

My appreciation goes to my mother, Barbara Almony, and father, Steve Hinds who each in their own way helped to make me the person I am today. I am thankful for my sisters, my nephews and nieces, my step-sister, step-brother, and of course my step-father Joe Almony. Some people are not lucky enough to have even one supportive parent and I was blessed with not only two wonderful parents, but an incredibly encouraging step-father as well. To all my friends, family, and loved ones you are all incredibly important to me. You are, each and every one, appreciated more than I can possibly say. I also thank every colleague and mentor I have had in my life and there have been many. Each of you has played a part in helping me to grow in different ways and I cannot thank you all enough.

Credit goes to Kay Gifford for taking the photo of me which is used on the cover of this book.

I want to thank Nathan Martin and the entire team at Sound Wisdom. Nathan, you not only encouraged me to write the book, but you were literally right there every step of the way making sure it made it from initial idea to reality. Your team has been absolutely amazing to work with and truly the experience has been one of the smoothest projects I have ever been involved with.

As I mentioned above, there are too many individual people who are deserving of personal acknowledgement to even attempt to list everyone individually. Therefore, please know that you are truly appreciated. I also want to thank you for not only reading this book, but for all the other ways you support the work I do. Whether by visiting the websites we run, as a newsletter reader, or attending one of the speaking events I have done. Please know that your support is appreciated more than I can possibly communicate here. Your support of my work is what allows me to

Acknowledgements

LIVE BIG in my life and for that dear friend I am grateful beyond words.

I would also like to thank Zig Ziglar for coining the phrase, "You can get everything in life you want if you help enough other people get what they want." That one little, yet powerful, quote has helped to shape my life in countless ways. I first read that when I was not much older than 15 years of age. I picked up my first personal development book and those words helped me realize that I should be a student of personal development ideas and having done so has paid numerous dividends throughout my life. My hope is that I can adequately impart some of those valuable lessons here in the pages of this book.

PROLOGUE

I've done this thousands of times before. Talking to prospective clients on the phone has always been a breeze. Where is this coming from? This crushing feeling... I just can't catch my breath and calm myself.

As if reading my mind, my client says, "It'll be OK, honey, take your time. Just take a minute to catch your breath..."

Wait a minute, I should be convincing her—not the other way around. What is going on? Why can't I talk?!

I had gone from being uncomfortable to bordering on extreme anxiety in no time flat. What started out as a normal day at the office had quickly deteriorated into what felt like one of the worst days of my life. I managed to struggle through the rest of the call before handing it off to a colleague to close the deal. I had never experienced anything like this before; but I knew, perhaps instinctively, that whatever I'd just felt is my "new norm."

Life is a journey, slapped full of ups and downs and all-arounds. We all have adversities throughout our life. At this particular moment in my life, I am experiencing adversity in the form of a symptom resultant from Tourette's syndrome. Tourette's syndrome is a neuropsychiatric disorder defined by its physical and vocal "tics". The tics are involuntary muscular actions that range from uncontrollable outbursts of screaming to simply eye blinking. It is diagnosed mainly in children and the symptoms generally wane as the child grows older. As a child, I was diagnosed with Tourette's and for the most part the symptoms had been fairly mild—until this disastrous phone call where I struggled with a symptom called a blocking tic. The best I can describe it is as the worst stutter you've ever heard—times about twenty. I can't spit out one word I want to say. Just beyond the vocal chords, which once worked flawlessly, with great skill even, something appears to hold me hostage from being able to communicate what I know in my mind I want to say. The more I try, the more frustrated I become—and, of course, the more frustrated I become, the more it grows into sheer anxiety. Despite the understanding of my client during this phone call, the increased anxiety exacerbated the blocking tic and I was rendered virtually speechless. That's a hard pill to swallow, and the experience would leave me with— among other things-- a phobia about doing business on the phone for years to come.

Just four years earlier, the summer before I turned sixteen, I had the opportunity to work in our family business. It was the start-up phase of the business, so there wasn't an abundance of extra resources to pay me. So my dad created a job for me. I was to call prospective clients, qualify them, and set up an appointment that I would turn over to one of our (more seasoned) salespeople who would then work the deal. If the deal closed, I received a portion of the sales commission.

As a fifteen year old, I didn't realize that this might not be the most desirable job. I saw it as an opportunity to succeed and make some money, so I dove in. I didn't stop to consider the challenges of the job, I didn't think of the things that might go wrong or the reasons why I shouldn't be any good at the job. Besides, I didn't know any other fifteen year old kids who got to go to work wearing a tie, sitting at a desk, and calling clients. To get anywhere, it takes action, so I picked up the phone and began my work. Soon I realized that I like this job, this challenge of making the sale. Over time, I became good at what I doing. I learned to use my voice and speech to affect positive responses from potential customers. I saw my future unfolding before me, and boy, was it ever bright!

Around this time, one of our salespeople took me aside one day and said, "Josh, you're doing well here, and over time and through trial and error, you will become even better. Or you can be proactive and hone your skill set by choice, and become better, sooner." To me at the time, it was a no-brainer—I wanted to get better, sooner. So I ran out to the bookstore that day after work and purchased a book by Zig Ziglar, a successful speaker and author. My study in personal development was under way. It was a good thing too, because I would need all the help I could get to deal with this new adversity.

This blocking tic is unpredictable. Just a few weeks after the embarrassing sales call, I went out on a date with a beautiful young lady. We had a wonderful dinner and saw a movie and enjoyed good conversation throughout the night. The next day I called to let her know I had a nice time on our date. I could not speak any of the words I was trying to say. Somehow I did manage to get to the point that she realized it was me on the phone; but beyond that, the call quickly deteriorated. I remember her saying, "If you really don't want to go out with me again, just let me know. You don't have to make up a fake stutter." It was a crushing experience, but one that I would experience on a number of different levels in the coming years.

As time went by, I remained in and out of the family business, never really excelling as I had early on—at least in the same context. I did, however, remain extremely interested in learning the skills I'd been a student of for so long—general business, entrepreneurship, sales, and communication. I practiced them as I learned them, mostly visualizing them.

Years later, things began to come into focus a bit more for me. Because I was interested in personal and professional development, I found myself looking for some way to express and unleash my passion for those topics. I found the answer when I found what is really a hobby website.

In 1996, while working with a local computer retailer, I purchased a domain name and a Web address. Initially, my idea was that I would do some basic computer tutoring and consulting on the local level. Because owning a domain name back then was trendy, I did just that. Looking back, it was sort of silly—why did I need a website to do local computer training—but hey, it was 1996.

About this same time, I came up with a simple little idea to create a Web page where I would link to specific Web pages for speakers and authors of whose work I am a fan. It wasn't some genius idea initially. Looking back, while I did a number of things wrong, one key thing I did correctly was that I got started on the idea. That is, I didn't wait for all the thoughts to start flooding in with all the reasons I shouldn't pursue the idea. I got started, and I enjoyed the process of breathing life into this idea.

At first, not a lot happened. I was thoroughly enjoying the project, but beyond that it wasn't as though I had some grand vision that in time it would become a full-time business that would eventually be responsible for me becoming a professional speaker. At the time I was working on the Web page this idea was so far out of the realm of my reality that if you'd have said it, I would have laughed right in your face…

So I gave my time to an idea—initially a simple idea, but one I was passionate about. I created a mission from that idea that is very much alive and serves to steer the direction our business follows to this day. That is: to offer the leading personal and professional development resources to people worldwide. Certainly it was an audacious goal when I first began. I didn't know exactly how I didn't go about making it a reality, so I just started out as best I could, very much like I had years before with my family's business.

Before long, interesting things began to happen. For starters, people actually started to visit the Web page. In fact, lots of them did. Soon the simple little Web page was included in the Yahoo Directory, in the self-improvement category. In the early days of the Web, most people used this directory, which was maintained by actual humans to surf and find things on the Web. There were more traditional search engines, but the Yahoo Directory was definitely a go-to resource for finding things. And someone, a real, live human being at Yahoo deemed my little hobby website to be worthy of being listed in the category; initially among twenty or so other related websites. Lots of people were visiting the site.

If you do your best, stay in the game, learn along the way, and adapt as best you can, life has an incredible way of filling in the details for you.

This is a profound lesson I learned and it describes how the business progressed from being a hobby to a formalized business. After more visitors began using the Website, several things became clear. I could keep things as they were, or I could ride this horse as best I could and see what might come about as a result.

I opted for the second choice; and years later, here I am with countless testimonials from people worldwide who have been positively impacted by that simple decision. My decision to give things a go, even though all the details for doing so weren't quite clear in the beginning, made all the difference. It's true that for the person willing to move forward in the pursuit of his or her dreams; the people, experiences, skills, and resources needed are revealed in due time.

Few worthwhile undertakings are easy. I'm certain that I've left far more than my fair share of money and opportunity on the table over the years, but I can say without a doubt that the journey and all that I have become as a result of having the courage to undertake the journey, far exceeds anything I could have hoped for.

Whatever particular frame of reference we choose to see our world through depends on our outlook. I have my high moments—and not-so-high moments. My outlook is that whatever life sends my way is an opportunity. I only need to understand this truth and then take action and I will eventually find success. Throughout this book, I reveal to you a number of different life lessons that have made a difference in my life—and I believe can do the same for you.

Prologue

Friend, you were made for greatness, and the way you honor that gift is by every single day moving forward, working at developing your talents and gifts. My hope for you is that the ideas in this book will serve to help you on that journey as you fully embrace and come to understand that this is your life, and as such it is your choice, a choice you must make through your actions every day to LIVE BIG!

1

DEFINING SUCCESS

Success means having the courage, the deter-
mination, and the will to become the person
you believe you were meant to be.

–George Sheehan

Define success. This is the obvious place to start, and based on the countless numbers of people I work with either through live trainings or one-on-one coaching, it is also the most often overlooked step. In most cases, it's not that they have completely neglected this step as much as they have done it half-heartedly.

Here's what I mean. When I ask people what success means to them, their answers are often along strictly monetary lines. Monetary rewards are only part of the success equation. You need to think in specific terms regarding what success means to you. Defining success helps you to better follow that moving target throughout your life. I've heard success defined as the freedom to be myself. Only the individual can honestly say what it would take in terms of free time, monetary freedom, or anything for that matter, to truly be his or her own self.

Mother Theresa was successful, I would say, in terms of the good works she did on behalf of some of the poorest people in the world. Parents who pour years of time, love, and energy into raising their children for the sake of watching them become all they can be are certainly successful. In both examples, the end result is of success and achievement without the acquisition of monetary wealth.

However you choose to define what it means to you to be successful and live a life of fulfillment, do yourself, your loved ones, and all those around you a favor and carefully create your own definition. As you fix that definition in your mind, you will put yourself in a position to attract that picture into your life. Live by choice rather than chance.

How Do You Measure Success?

My feeling is that as long as I have the resources necessary to move through life fully able to pursue the goals and dreams that are important to me, then I am successful. This definition gives us the room to dream and really think about what it would take to live out our goals and dreams— the things that we truly place personal value on—not just those things that outside forces may deem important such as money or material possessions.

Say, for example, you want to be the best parent you can be. That doesn't take a lot of money, does it? No. Unless you think to be a good parent you must have ample amounts of money to care for your children. In this case, it is not the amount of money you have or lack. In fact, only you can decide what is enough for you and your loved ones.

It is far easier to take our due credit for our past achievements when we're not holding ourselves up to someone else's standard. Competition isn't a bad thing, but when it's the only measuring stick we use, it can end up working against us if we are not careful.

In my opinion, success is best measured on a personal level. When we frame what constitutes living a successful life around those things that we personally see as valuable, then we enjoy where we are now more. Life will offer up opportunities to us that we never noticed before.

When we set out to do the best we can do, it is inevitable that great opportunity finds us because we are doing what truly makes us happy. We're in alignment and ready for the opportunities that life puts in our path.

Keep this thought in mind: success is a personal thing. Define it according to what you value most, and you are far more likely to achieve it as well as enjoy it once you have it.

THE SUCCESS JOURNEY STARTS WITH YOU

As Henry David Thoreau so eloquently wrote, *"Most people lead lives of quiet desperation and go to the grave with the song still in them."* Many people miss the mark, not because they lack the ability to achieve success in their given endeavors, but rather because they never take the time to truly identify what success means to them. And as a result, they end up moving aimlessly through life hoping to hit upon what it is they think they want to achieve—often not even truly realizing what it is they are seeking.

When you have a solid definition of success crafted, you can use it to lay out a plan to follow that will naturally put you in alignment with whatever it is that you believe to be most important. I have had conversations with people who, after taking the time to define what success means to them personally, realized in that very moment that they had many times already experienced great success in their lives.

I'm fond of the saying, "success begets success," which in its simplest form means that one achievement—no matter how small it may appear at the time—allows us to build upon that achievement and move forward to the next task, which upon completion, will propel us further on to our next undertaking. Hence, success begets success. Or, one successful outcome leads to greater accomplishments.

It Doesn't Always Take Money, Honey!

Some of the greatest success stories ever told are about people just like you and I who started with little or nothing and grew their business idea into a masterful success. Would it have been easier if these folks had access to deep pockets when starting out on their business journey? Maybe, maybe not—who knows for sure. One could make the case that in some of the situations had these bootstrapping entrepreneurs had it easier at startup, many of them would never have learned the value of persistence and the necessity to be creative in growing their businesses in the first place.

So my question now is what are you waiting for? It's your life that's waiting for you, why not get the ball rolling now, take a little action, and start moving toward the success that awaits you?

If you have yet to clearly define what success means to you, take the time to do that now. Be sure that your definition is highly personal. Acknowledge times in your life when you have met with positive outcomes.

When you have your personal definition of success, you will have a powerful road map from which you can make decisions—you have a gauge from which you can look at potential goals and ideas and measure the commitment it will take to see them through to completion based on those things that are most important to you.

In some instances, you may find that a given undertaking isn't really in alignment with your definition of success and that even if you were to achieve a goal that it wouldn't move you closer to what you personally define as leading a successful life. At other times, it will be crystal clear that your current endeavor, the path you find yourself on, is totally in line with what you've taken the time to define as being successful after you've compared it to what you've identified.

ACTION STEPS

1. Take the time right now to get clear on what success means to you. What will it look like? What will it feel like? What things are truly most important to you? What resources will be available to you when you are leading a truly successful life? What difference will having those resources available to you make not only in your life, but in the lives of those around you—family, friends, co-workers, etc.?

2. Each morning before you begin your day, recite to yourself your personal definition of success. Close your eyes as you recite it to yourself and take a moment to think about what it will be like when you are truly living your own definition of success. Consider any actions that you must take in order to move yourself closer to whatever you define as successful. See yourself doing those things with ease—and as you're doing so, moving closer to whatever it is you have identified.

For these two steps to work, you need to create a habit for doing them. At first, it may appear that you aren't being authentic, or you may even feel that you're telling yourself a lie. The main thing is to do it anyway. It may not feel authentic because it's something you may not be used to doing. Think about the first time you learned to ride a bike. You had to tell yourself that you would learn to ride it. You had to instill the belief that you could do it, which eventually led you to a point where you were able to do it with ease.

Through this simple, daily exercise, you will develop the positive habit of keeping your own definition of success nearby at all times, which will ensure that you are working on and staying plugged into what is necessary to fully live your own definition of success.

LIVE BIG:
MOVE TOWARD YOUR DREAMS

"Life rewards those who aren't afraid to step out in the direction of their dreams. I am that person. Today and every day from now on I am claiming the dreams I have for myself. I am more than capable of achieving whatever I want in my life. What skills I lack now I can learn. Through action I am making progress daily."

"Keep steadily before you the fact that all true success depends at last upon yourself."
–Theodore T. Hunger

Defining success and owning your personal vision of success is step number one in learning to LIVE BIG!

2

GOAL SETTING

"The major reason for setting a goal is for what it makes of you to accomplish it. What it makes of you will always be the far greater value than what you get."

–Jim Rohn

Consider the definition of success that you outlined in Chapter 1 from an imagined 10,000 foot aerial view. In Chapter 2, your boots are on the ground and you're looking at an up-close and personal action plan for making what you want--your success definition-- into what you have!

Before we go any further, right now, stop reading, close your eyes, and take several deep breaths. Just clear your mind as best you can, and take a few breaths. Done? Good. Now here's what you must absolutely understand if what

I'm going to share with you in this most important of lessons is going to help you. Make no mistake, if you get this, it will help you tremendously going forward.

Drum roll, please.

Virtually everything you want to achieve, have ever achieved in the past, or will accomplish in the future depends on your ability to keep it front and center of mind to the point that you will work on it until you meet with success.

Why is that so important? Because unless you understand and adopt this truth into your goal-setting programs, you will not get the results that you would if you were to embrace this idea. The saying, "out of sight, out of mind," describes well the goal-killing truth of losing visual representation of your goals. Keep clearly in mind the following truth: the things we keep foremost in our mind get our attention, and whatever gets our attention, gets done!

If you find that what you are doing regarding setting goals isn't working, then read on because the following goal-setting plan is a simple and effective way to increase your success in achieving your goals.

THE GOAL CARDS SYSTEM

This is a particular goal-setting system that I call the Goal Cards System—GCS, not GPS although it does show you where you're going. I teach it as a workshop or in presentations and live trainings that I present to businesses and organizations. When I'm teaching it live, it's a lot more interactive; but since we don't have that luxury here, I'm going to give you the steps involved so that you can put it to work and benefit from doing so in your own personal and professional life.

The system is built around the idea that you can have the very best of intentions, but unless your goal-setting plan includes in it a strong component for keeping you plugged into and working on the things you have deemed most important, it's going to be difficult for you to achieve what you want to see come to fruition in your life. On the other hand, if you employ a system like the one I'm about to share with you and use it on a consistent basis, you will see the goals you set come to fruition.

The Goal Cards System is simple by design. It consists in its simplest form of only a few things:

- 3x5 index cards
- A universal binder clip (sometimes referred to as a bull clip, think heavy duty paper)
- The steps — detailed below
- Your willingness and commitment to keep your goal cards nearby, always, and work on their completion.

So there you have it, you likely already have all that's needed to use the system to its fullest — without having to buy anything. And if you do, it is a very minimal investment on your part.

I teach this system using 3x5 index cards, but you can use another medium if you so desire. In fact, you could use a combination of a smart phone (Blackberry, iPhone, etc.) and 3x5 cards. I teach it using 3x5 index cards for a few reasons: One, I started teaching it that way years ago. Two, teaching it using just 3x5 index cards proves that getting started is simple and doesn't require a large investment, beyond your honest commitment. Three, it's very easy to take a group or audience through the set-up in that format.

I should also mention that after you understand the format and steps of the system, you will realize that it's the principles of the system that make it effective more than the particular medium. In short, it's all about keeping what you want front and center of mind, which inevitably helps to ensure you see more of those things and experiences coming to pass in your life.

Here is an example Goal Card you can use, along with a description of how you can use it to achieve your heart's desires.

MY GOAL CARD

Main Goal/Objective: _____

_____

_____

_____

_____

Date and Targeted Time for Completion:

_____

Action Steps: Be sure to use real actions that, when completed, will move you closer to success on the "main goal/objective" listed at the top of each particular Goal Card. This part of the Goal Card is an ongoing process. New action steps are added as they are identified, and as existing action steps are completed (each day if necessary). This is necessary because it keeps you actively plugged in and taking action on what is necessary to get you to where you want to be.

Example:

_____Action Item Number 1
_____Action Item Number 2

Personalized Statement of why you want to achieve the particular goal you have set.

Written from the heart, highly personal. The idea is that when you read this section it will rekindle your inner motivation for why you want to put forth all the effort that is necessary to accomplish this particular endeavor.

Hopefully you have found this generic example Goal Card helpful. The following actual card may be even more helpful.

TAYLOR'S GOAL CARD

Main Goal/Objective: To save enough money to add another bedroom and bathroom.

Date and Targeted Time for Completion: December 2013.

Action Steps:

_____ Look for part-time work that won't interfere with family time and day job.

_____ Ask family what they are willing to give up to increase savings.

_____ Research to find the best builders: Internet, friends, Better Business Bureau, etc.

_____ Request quotes from multiple builders.

_____ Compare costs against the increase in property value.

_____ Determine how much we need to set aside each payday toward the goal.

_____ Inquire about bartering services.

_____ Watch for sales on items needed for the project.

Why I want to achieve this goal: Our three daughters have to share one bedroom, and all five of us have to share one bathroom. They don't have enough closet space or room to do their homework. Getting ready for work and school in the morning is hard for the entire family with only one bathroom. I want to accomplish this goal to make our family life more enjoyable.

This example may not be close to what you consider a goal, but to some families, this would be a major and welcomed achievement. Your first card may involve the steps you need to take to earn your college degree or become an apprentice. Your goal may be to become more involved in your child's school, start your own business, or earn a promotion at work. Maybe you would like to lose 50 pounds or play an instrument. Remember, your goals are directly tied to your personal definition of success. The system is a way to keep your goals visible and real.

Often I use both 3x5 cards and my cell phone to set reminders for myself, reminders using the outline and steps mentioned. The point isn't to get caught up in the details of the "right or wrong" way to do this as much as it is to adapt it to your own style—one that you will actually use. You have to stay plugged into and working on the things you have said are worth your effort if you want to see them manifest. You have to be in it to win it!

You must also remember that the Goal Cards System works because it's a "living system". By that I mean it requires your ongoing participation, especially in the form of the Action Steps section. If you're working at the system, you will be spending the bulk of your time accomplishing, planning, rewriting new action steps, and then getting back to work on the new actions you come up with. That's very much an ongoing process. That's the glue of the system.

Another key reason to keep your goals and action steps visible is that when you feel a sense of accomplishment, even a minimal amount at the time, it creates a snowball effect that encourages you to do more, which in turn leads to even greater results. So staying "in the game" gives you a sense of accomplishment that keeps your progress moving forward.

As I often say, personal development is a hands-on project—you have the BIGGEST part in your own growth. If you use the Goal Cards System as a regular part of your daily routine, it will serve you greatly. You will quickly start to see more of your goals and desires becoming achievements and proud accomplishments.

MOVE FORWARD CONFIDENTLY

Make action your ally as you move confidently in the direction of the goals you set. Take ample time to evaluate the steps to ensure they are in fact moving you in the right direction.

Friend, actions in and of themselves won't guarantee that you will meet your desired outcome. Right action is needed. Consider the following example: If you practice a certain incorrect technique to the point that it becomes a habit, you will unfortunately have learned to do that thing the wrong way. It could be a tennis swing or golf stroke, for instance. The solution is to make sure you're learning the right way and taking actions accordingly. In doing so, you'll develop habits that will serve you going forward. Remember, practice makes permanent, but perfect practice makes perfect.

KEEP THE KINKS OUT OF YOUR GOAL-SETTING PLAN

When it comes to achieving your goals, keep in mind that old saying, "out of sight, out of mind." Anytime we allow ourselves to lose sight of our desired goal, it can end up creating a real kink in the goal-setting process. Our lives can and will get hectic. If we take our eyes off what we want, life has a way of putting some other action that requires our attention in its place.

It's really that simple.

So what's the solution? Keep lists, to-do lists, actions tasks—whatever you choose to call them. The point is to keep your goals nearby and in plain sight. And just as important, also write down the smaller tasks that support you in reaching your larger goals—even if that includes going to bed early one night because you have a critical meeting the next day.

Keep yourself on the correct path by taking time to evaluate where you are now and exactly what you want to accomplish. By making certain you are doing what's needed, and putting forth the effort required of you to achieve what you have committed to accomplishing, you will find that you are moving with confidence in the direction of your heart's desire.

PAST ACHIEVEMENTS PROVIDE FUEL FOR CURRENT GOALS

Allow your past achievements to provide fuel for your current goals. Because you're reading this right now, I have a strong suspicion that you believe wholeheartedly in the importance of goal setting and planning for the future. For this I congratulate you!

That said, do you give equal time to reflect on just how far you have come? Do you celebrate the successes and life achievements you have had? In doing this, you will find a wonderful source of motivation and strength. This is validation that can move you more swiftly along the path of your current plan.

Keeping your motivational batteries charged is essential. Tapping into your past achievements is an easy and extremely effective way to recharge your confidence, which provides you with what's needed to charge full steam ahead in the lofty pursuit of your dreams.

DON'T JUST CHECK IT OFF— MARK IT DONE!

Mark it done! After finishing a task, we often feel the immediate need to literally strike that task off our list. While this is normal, it may be far better to follow the idea that a reader of my newsletter sent in to me: Rather than simply "striking it off the list," this person chose to mark it done!

On the surface we might not see much of a difference. However, by marking it "done," it is easier to look back on our achievements and see the progress we've made in our efforts.

Take the time to write down and track your daily accomplishments. Doing so will greatly help to guide you in the direction of your goals and dreams, that does wonders toward making them realities.

Always keep firmly in mind that we create our own luck through a four letter word, "work" and six letter word, "effort."

ACTION STEP

Briefly write out your goals—take the time to do this at least once a day! In doing so, you will find a terrific way to reconnect with them. Make no mistake, keeping them front and center in your life helps you see them through. Repetition is definitely your friend when it comes to goal achievement.

LIVE BIG:
GOAL SETTING AND ACHIEVING

"I have within me the ability to achieve whatever worthwhile goal I set my mind to accomplish. Whatever I may lack in skill, I can learn. The fact that others with seemingly far less in the way of resources have reached their definition of success is proof positive that I can as well. Through persistence, a willingness to learn what is needed, and the honest commitment toward taking daily action on moving in the direction I want my life to go, I am crafting the life of my dreams. I don't ask for an easy road, I ask for the persistence and willingness to trudge ahead when necessary. In doing so, I'm assured that I will achieve my desired destination. Success is part of who I am."

LIVE BIG:
GOAL VISUALIZATION

"I am vigilant when it comes to working on the goals I have for myself. I keep in mind the old saying, 'Out of sight, out of mind.' I write down and schedule times when I will work on the things I've identified as worthwhile to pursue. Each of us has 24 hours in a day, if one person is capable of using that number of hours to pursue their goals, then I, too, can find the time to do so. I resist the natural human urge to accept excuses that attempt to convince me of all the reasons I'm too busy. The simple truth is, I may very

well be busy, life may be moving 90 to nothing, but the fact remains that if I want to reach my intended destination, I have to work within the allotted time each day. I'm going to adjust and give ample time toward achieving the success I desire. I am as capable as anyone when it comes to manifesting my dreams. Through persistence, action, and holding on to the vision of what success means to me, I am moving confidently in the direction of all the rewards life has in store for me."

Satisfaction lies in the effort not the attainment. Full effort is full victory."

–Mahatma Ghandi

Set your goals, plan the proper action to attain them, keep them in sight, and get ready to Live BIG!

3

VISUALIZATION

"Visualize this thing that you want, see it, feel it, believe in it. Make your mental blue print, and begin to build."

–Robert Collier

Have you ever watched athletes just before they take part in an athletic event or competition? I've noticed that they close their eyes, seem to take a breath, and then are still for a moment. If you've ever watched the Olympic Games, there's a better than average chance you've seen many of those athletes practicing what is referred to as visualization. It's just what it sounds like.

Athletes actually run through their minds the successful outcome they desire. Of course visualization isn't something only for world class athletes. It can and often is used to achieve all sorts of goals and positive outcomes.

The Collins English Dictionary defines visualization as: "a technique involving focusing on positive mental images in order to achieve a particular goal." Now with our subject clearly defined, we move forward into the discussion on the many benefits of using visualization.

Fuel to Achieve Your Wildest Dreams and Aspirations

It is said that the mind can't differentiate between a vividly imagined experience and a real one. It is for this reason that many people ranging from athletes to business people, actors, entertainers, and everyday people use visualization to create a mental image of what they want to achieve. Then they play that image through their minds at different points during the day.

Repetition of an activity can help us internalize what's involved in accomplishing the thing and the careful use of visualization, assuming that we're playing out the activity vividly and correctly in our minds, can help add to the activity we want to master. This idea may be a little far-fetched to you, particularly if you're not a person who makes it part of your daily routine; but suffice it to say that you wouldn't see so many world class Olympic athletes using visualization if it didn't produce winning results.

Notice that I'm not suggesting that visualization alone will do the trick. It won't. But it can be an important part of the goal setting and achievement puzzle if you use it. Action, as we've covered already is key, that's a given; but visualization can help us experience (in our powerful minds) that we're taking the positive actions necessary to get us to where we want to be.

There's more than one way to visualize. Often people will say to me that they can't visualize their goals effectively. They don't feel as though they can vividly see their goals and the steps necessary enough to be effective

First, we have to keep in mind that there are three basic learning styles: visual, auditory, and kinesthetic. So for people who are highly visual, they may have no problem whatsoever closing their eyes, taking a deep breath, and running an image through their minds that appears as vivid as a movie. Yet, for people who are more auditory, they might not get the same effect taking the more traditional visual approach. They would likely be much better off introducing sounds or visualizing from an auditory perspective, focusing on words and sounds in their minds. They may even need to make a recording of their particular goal by reading their "visualization" so they can play it back and listen to it.

You may need to adapt how your methods until you find a combination that's best for you. I like to think of the time I spend visualizing as "practicing" in my mind.

For example, since part of my business involves giving live presentations and trainings to groups and organizations, I have to practice to stay proficient. While I certainly run through my presentation in the more traditional manner, practicing in front of the mirror, or running through a lecture in front of an imaginary audience, I make use of visualization as well. In my mind, I see myself as vividly as possible sharing my presentation. I envision members of the audience sitting on the edge of their seats. I hear and see the applause. I visualize the positive outcome I want to receive. Making that a regular part of my routine has helped me tremendously since I began doing it many years ago.

The opportunities to visualize positive outcomes for yourself are limitless. Some examples: a conversation with a prospective client, asking your employer for a raise, convincing yourself you have what it takes to go after your dreams, and anything in between.

Just as you stay on a solid exercise program and begin to see your muscles build, so you will start to see the positive effects of your time spent visualizing begin to come to fruition. The important thing is that you stick with your commitment to visualizing long enough to see its many benefits kick in for you. Have a little faith that it will work for you, and in time, you will see it do so.

EFFECTIVE VISUALIZATION

Here is a quick overview to help you set the stage for effective visualization:

1. Close your eyes.
2. Take several deep breaths.
3. Let go of negative thoughts
4. Imagine—in detail—yourself achieving goals with the most positive outcome possible.

If you are more visual in nature, then see it as best you can. If you can't vividly see it in your mind, simply imagine it in a way that works for you. Hear it, as though it were a story being told to you. Mix up your visualization a bit and introduce all three elements if that works for you: kinesthetic, auditory, and visual.

Practice these steps daily and you will quickly begin to experience the benefits that many successful people know and enjoy.

Remember, no one can put the ideas you're learning in this book to use for you. That's a decision and commitment you have to make. Any number of the ideas you are learning can have a tremendous impact on your personal and professional life, but you have to put them to use on a daily basis.

MENTAL MOVIES TO START YOUR DAY

If you're like most people, you hop right out of bed each morning without giving much thought to it. Instead, consider taking just a few extra minutes to set the tone for your day by mentally running through the positive outcomes you want to experience. Run through the goals you're currently working on.

In your mind, play out a mental movie of yourself doing the steps and accomplishing whatever is required of you to see things through. Fully experience the sense of accomplishment and fulfillment you will have as a result of achieving the things you're currently working on.

Starting your day with a little visualization of the things you want in life can be a simple, yet highly effective way to ensure you stay plugged into and focused on what you want to achieve. As Napoleon Hill, author of *Think and Grow Rich* wrote, "What the mind of man can conceive and believe it can achieve."

The point is that you're giving thought to what you want to see come to fruition in your life as opposed to taking the route that many folks do—simply hoping things will work out.

Remember, we are inclined to put work into things that have the most of our attention, and the things we work on lead to a greater sense of accomplishment. The simple strategy outlined above is easy to do, but it's also easy not to do. The choice is yours!

A BRAND NEW DAY

Whatever happened yesterday, good or bad, is now rooted in the past.

In the moment in which we now find ourselves, we have the ability to focus in on and do the things that serve us for the better—or we can give our attention to those things that reignite whatever thoughts that cause us to remain stuck in the moment or the past.

We have a choice; and fortunately, it isn't all that difficult to set the tone early on in your day. Does that mean you are guaranteed not to meet with a challenge early on that will knock you off course or throw you for a loop? Of course not, but in the event that something (or someone) shows up with such an agenda, you will find yourself more prepared to deal with it and able to adjust course accordingly.

Here are four simple but effective ideas you can use to start your day on a positive note.

1. *Upon waking, name at least ten people for whom you are thankful.* Recount those in your life who have had a positive impact on you. Think of those who have in some way helped to make you the unique person you are. Don't sell yourself short. No matter what place you may find yourself right now, you are still an amazing person with unique gifts and talents. You don't have to believe it, but it's still the absolute truth! Practicing gratitude is a powerful thing that helps to reconnect you with your inner power and the abilities that make up who you are.

2. *Give thanks for your talents and skills.* You have been blessed with special skills and talents. You may not feel as though you've completely developed them all up to this point in your life, but that doesn't change the fact that you have them. Think through those things that others compliment you on, those are talents. Don't underestimate all the amazing bits and pieces

that go into making you the person you are. As you identify and give thanks for the talents that were bestowed upon you, commit to developing them and becoming more proficient in their use.

3. *Before going to bed, write down the most important action steps you will take the next day.* The simple act of writing down the next day's most important tasks will give you a plan to move on. Keep in mind that you can get the most productive mileage if you put your "super tasks" at the top so you can complete them first. Consider super tasks as those things that upon completion will give you the absolute most bang for your buck. Consider the difference between a super task and one of lesser importance. A super task might be calling on a prospective client while a normal task may be to cut the grass. While both are important, and you want to complete both, first example is going to lead toward a greater reward. When possible, concentrate on the super tasks that move you forward at a maximum pace. Another such super task might be to spend time studying your industry or chosen profession.

4. *In the morning, review the actions steps you wrote down the night before.* As you are looking over the items you wrote down, close your eyes and see yourself completing them and experiencing the wonderful sense of accomplishment for having done so. After you have visualized yourself finishing the items on your daily action list, take a deep breath and begin your day working on and completing

them. Keep in mind that each new day is an opportunity to implement daily actions that can steer your life in the direction you want it to go. You can sail your ship, or choose to remain mired in inaction and float aimlessly, dependent upon whatever life may throw your way. My sincere hope for you is that you will choose the first option.

ACTION STEP

Review the four ideas offered to help you start each and every day in a forward, proactive movement. Decide now to commit to these ways, to improve your progress toward your goal.

LIVE BIG:
SET THE TONE OF YOUR DAY

"The way I choose to start my day sets its tone. When I make the decision to begin by giving thanks for the positive things in my life, no matter how seemingly few or bountiful they might be, I am setting the flow for new opportunities to come my way. Each and every day I will remind myself that I can steer my outcome in any direction I wish, by the actions I take. The steps I take day in and day out are the determining factors as to whether or not I achieve the success I desire. I take comfort in knowing that I have control over the actions I choose to do or not do."

LIVE BIG:
ABOUT CREATIVITY

"Each day I am allowing my creativity to flow—bringing forth ideas that I can put into play that will lead me in a positive direction on the path toward

achieving my given endeavors. I take special care not to suppress my creativity, and act on opportunities that present themselves to allow my creative side to shine through in my daily life. In doing so, I am allowing myself to grow for the betterment of all involved."

"Throughout the centuries there were men who took first steps, down new roads, armed with nothing but their own vision."

–Ayn Rand

Use your imagination to see the ways in which you will achieve your goals and Live BIG!

4

PERSISTENCE

"Great works are performed not by strength but by perseverance."

–Samuel Johnson

When we hear others share their story, the triumphs and challenges, the high and lows, we often miss an important point. We miss that while the retelling of the story sounds like things were fast-paced and exciting, the truth is, often the BIGGEST difference between the successful person and the unfulfilled person is the amount of time each spends on those sometimes mundane activities that are required to make progress.

It's true that sometimes the success journey is boring. It's the commitment to keep working on those seemingly unimportant activities, those often small steps that ulti-mately lead us to achieving our larger plan

STICK-TO-IT-NESS

Friend, if you long to increase your income over the next year, you are likely going to have to do more connecting with and reaching out to customers and prospects. Those are the activities that I'm talking about. If you want to achieve your larger destination, you've got to know what activities and steps you can take on a consistent basis that will get you there. Then you've got to move forward with an unwavering stick-to-it-ness until you achieve what you put your mind to.

When you study the lives of those who are moving their dreams into reality, you find that it isn't because they are more gifted or talented; rather, they shrink the gap between the amount of time it takes them to formulate their ideas, put them into practice, and begin taking real solid action.

The world is full of well-intentioned people. If you can make a habit of taking your ideas from intention and turning them into actionable steps sooner than later, you will find yourself well ahead of those who remain stuck in the dream state. It's not nearly as important to have every single detail hammered out before getting started. In fact, in my experience, waiting to get started can be a determining factor as to whether or not you ever do get started. Not because your intentions aren't well-meaning, but because there will always be something else that will pop up and vie for your attention. And as we know so well, whatever gets our attention, more often than not tends to get done.

Therefore, you must accept that ultimately it's your choice as to what you make room for and give your attention to. Always ask, "Is this thing I'm working on and giving my attention to serving to move me in the direction I want my life to go?" If you keep this question clearly in mind, act accordingly on the answer that comes to mind, and practice persistence on an ongoing basis, you will find that your life will become one of greater fulfillment and abundant achievement.

I like the quote from Winston Churchill, "Success is not final, failure is not fatal: it is the courage to continue that counts."

APPLYING THE BROKEN WINDOW THEORY

The Broken Window Theory comes from ideas included in an article titled "Broken Windows" by James Q. Wilson and George L. Kelling, which originally appeared in the magazine *The Atlantic Monthly*. Later, a book was published that adapted the ideas shared in the original article.

The theory goes like this: If a building has a few broken windows and they aren't repaired in a timely fashion, the tendency is for vandals to break even more windows. If time continues without the windows being fixed (the perception is that no one really cares), they might even break into the building and over time do far greater harm or destruction.

There are several different examples that point to the idea that when people care, or are taking notice of the "small things," it's that much easier to keep the "BIG things" in check. The broken windows theory has more than its share of proponents for and against its validity. In fact, you can see for yourself by searching the Internet for "broken windows theory." My point here is not to take a stand for or against it. Rather, my intent is to explore ways that we can apply and benefit from it in our lives.

The broken windows theory can be a catalyst for personal growth. Consider the idea that if personal and professional things go unchecked, undone, and uncorrected over a length of time, it's likely that a person will continue on the path they're on—regardless of whether the path leads to a destination of success and fulfillment. It kind of makes you think doesn't it?

I believe that it is the little things, the time we take to actually set goals and plan the actions to achieve those goals that matter greatest. As does our actually following through and taking the steps to complete the actions we've identified as most important. You see, we can't simply wish for things to change—we have to be active and persistent participants in whatever change we wish to manifest in our lives.

Fortunately, it doesn't require monumental amounts of action to initiate change. In the case of your life, you can begin the process by implementing on a consistent basis a few things that include, but are by no means limited to, the following suggestions.

Beginning the process requires considering some of the "broken windows" in your life that you can "fix" ongoing—and in turn begin to facilitate greater personal growth:

Take control of the way you begin your day. Barring the truly ultra-rare instances in our lives when we are faced with things that simply take time to work past (loss of a loved one, for example), for the most part, if we are honest with ourselves, we would have to admit that a good night's sleep has the power to start us fresh and ready for the next day. The challenge comes in when we begin the day giving very little thought to planning and committing to see the good things that will inevitably come to us during the day. Usually when we wake up, the day is neutral. But then the things we allow into our world and our minds early on tend to lead to us into a positive or negative attitude. Hence, if the first thing you focus on are the terrible events of yesterday and all the things that didn't go your way, you will begin to experience more of the same during the new day.

The same, of course, is true for the person who proactively introduces or focuses on yesterday's positives—
yesterday's wins, as I like to call them. That's not to say it
doesn't require a certain amount of work, or that we will
ever achieve a point in which a negative thought, or as Zig
Ziglar calls it, "stinking thinking," won't appear. However,
because we are aware of it when it does, we can choose to
shift our thoughts to ones that can serve us in some way and
build us up.

Here are a few more simple steps to help you take control of your day:

- Give thanks for the events and people who have
  had a positive impact on your life, either from
  your past or present.

- Read or listen to something of a positive nature.
  If the first thing you're kicking your day off
  with has the remote possibility of making you
  feel badly, make a different choice! That's not
  to say you have to run around avoiding any and
  all news sources—I'm not arguing for or against
  that—I am suggesting that it's not the very first
  way to begin your day. You can choose to set
  the tone of your day. If you don't at least try,
  you have no one but yourself to blame. After
  all, what do you really have to lose in trying this
  simple approach?

- Keep a Success Journal. I'm not talking about a
  diary in which you write down everything about
  your life—the good, the bad, and dare I say the
  things you view as downright dreadful. For our
  purposes, we only include positive experiences,
  the day-to-day wins. You can, of course, include
  your goals, long-term, short-term, and any term

in between. To put it as plainly as I can, only record things and events in your Success Journal that can serve you and help you develop into a better you in some way. In doing so, you create a very real source of positive validation for yourself. Whenever you find yourself doubting your ability, you can look back over your Journal and see firsthand that you have plenty to celebrate. It can also make for a terrific storehouse of ideas from which you can refer to and tap back into as you go forward.

- Ponder, write down, and act on your goals. Here is a favorite quote from speaker and author Susan Jeffers, "Feel the fear, and do it anyway." It always reminds me of the importance and inner power that comes from applying forward momentum to a thing or idea.

I'm often amazed by how easily we humans can get excited by and motivated to see a thing through, simply by having the initiative to get started. It's like a campfire—without the initial effort that goes into starting it, no amount of wishing otherwise is going to get those hot dogs cooked or needed warmth provided. Yet, once the fire has started, it takes very little if any additional effort to keep it going.

I hope that you will consider putting to use a few of the ideas in this chapter, or if you're up to the challenge give them all a shot! Consider also what an impact seeing things through the lens of the broken window theory might have for you. Inaction, if left unchecked, can leave you running the risk of things escalating in a direction that you might not otherwise choose for yourself. Keep that in mind and be ever on the lookout for positive habits you can apply and put to work in your life.

THE MAGIC QUESTION

Sometimes you will find yourself on top of the world, at other times you may feel as though the weight of the world is crashing down upon you. And yet at other times, you may find yourself somewhere in between, hopefully in a place much closer to the former than the latter.

Yes, life is a moving target. It has its twists, turns, ups and downs, but all in all, even the most difficult challenges can serve us and make us better in some way, provided we are willing to accept it to be true. Even if it is simply the growth which can come from realizing how powerful we are for having overcome the given challenge in the first place.

The essential thing to remember when you find yourself going through life's turmoils is to avoid the temptation to think that life, or depending on where you are in terms of your faith, that God is somehow trying to keep you down. That's the easy route, to accept that something or someone outside of yourself is trying to keep you from the good things in life. Resist that line of thinking with all your might; for in accepting such thinking, you lose your inner power that can only be fully ignited when you ask the magic question, "What in this situation can I control?"

It's a simple question, but when you ask it of yourself, and genuinely think it through, the answer that comes to you is so empowering! You see, being stuck and feeling as though things are out of your control is an incredibly dis-empowering place to be. It has the power to make us feel that no matter what we try, no matter what we do, we're stuck; nothing is working. When we are in that place mentally, we can become consumed by that line of thinking and even begin to believe that it's true.

On the other hand, there is always, in even the most seemingly desperate of situations some action that, if taken and acted upon, will give you the ability to move you from that place of desperation to where you want to be.

The key is being able to block out the stinking thinking long enough to ask and answer the all-important question, "What can I control in this situation?" When the answer comes to you, and it will, don't over-think it, don't fall victim to that inner voice that pleads its case as to all the reasons your solution won't possibly work. Instead, get into action as soon as humanly possible.

THE LAW OF DIMINISHING INTENT

The reason kicking into action is so vital is that the Law of Diminishing Intent is real. This law states simply that the longer it takes for you to begin an activity, the more likely you will be to never get started in the first place—and as a result, you never see the positive results you would have had you simply gotten started. Believe me, it's real, and you will find yourself its victim if you don't adopt the habit of moving forward in action as quickly as humanly possible.

To help you become a "do it now" person, keep in mind this small short but mighty mantra that speaker and author Brian Tracy suggests, "Do it now, do it now, do it now." Simple, but simple works!

If you have heard one of my speaking presentations or happen to have followed my work for any amount of time, you've probably heard me say, "You can't always control what happens to you in life, but you can always control how you react to what happens to you." For example, if you've been laid off from your job—no matter how much you think about it, at the end of the day, you're still out of a job. But the way you choose to react to that unfortunate situation is in your control. You can choose to double up on the number of resumes you send out, attend networking events, letting those in attendance know you're available for employment, search the newspaper and the Internet, etc. Notice that I recognize your unfortunate situation, but that there are actions you can control that will secure you another job. No amount of thought you give about what is or isn't fair will serve you.

However, what can work for you is choosing to react, take some action that can move you into a more positive direction. Asking the Magic Question will get you on the path to where you want to go.

While I used the example of a job loss above, you could easily replace it with the challenge of not making a sale, or having family or relationship challenges. Any number of things could be substituted in the example. The point isn't to act as though everything in life is all roses all the time. Sometimes we all experience very real, very hard challenges. It's part of the human experience.

Keep clearly in mind that you are an incredible person with amazing gifts and talents. Whatever challenges you may be facing or have faced in your past are not your reality. You can work through them and overcome them. As you move through your day, weeks, and the years ahead, develop the helpful habit of asking the magic question, "What can I control in this situation?"

CHOOSE PURPOSE OVER CHANCE

As you move through your day, remember that you can either operate by chance, or with purpose. Chance is certainly one choice, but the end result never works out as well as deciding on purpose. Beginning the journey of living on purpose can be as simple as taking the time each night to write down some necessary tasks or items that when completed will get you to where you want to go in life. In the grand scheme of things, the time it takes to develop that habit is nothing compared to the vast benefits you'll gain as a result. Make the choice to live on purpose over chance.

ACTION STEP

Write down a time when, against all odds, you persevered and were victorious—no matter how small or great the experience. Bask in your accomplishment for a while. Then write down an obstacle you are facing that makes you want to give up. Consider all your options and write down five reasons why you should stick to it.

LIVE **BIG:**
SUCCESS THROUGH PERSISTENCE

"As I focus and take action on the things that give me a sense of joy, great opportunity finds me. I am as capable of achieving my heart's desires as anyone else. If one person can succeed in the pursuit of his or her dreams, then I accept that as proof positive that I can as well. I work diligently day in and day out on the vision I have for myself, both personally and professionally. In doing so, I am crafting my ideal life."

LIVE **BIG:**
HOLDING TIGHTLY TO YOUR VISION

"I hold tightly to the vision of what I want to accomplish. I leave little to chance because I have a plan that outlines not only where I want to end up in life, but how to go about getting there. Because I make the trait of stick-to-it-ness my ally, I will outlast those who give up or quit before experiencing the sweet rewards of success. I embrace and make my mantra, 'slow and steady wins the race.' If I happen to experience accelerated success, the more the

better; but I don't require it nor do I give up if things take time. I was made for greatness, and every day I strive to live my life to the fullest."

Live **BIG:**
Persistence and Strong Determination

"My allies are persistence and strong determination to achieve my endeavors when faced with life's challenges. Through my willingness to stay in the game and learn what needs to be learned, I am moving myself ever closer toward attaining my own definition of success—however I may choose to define it."

"Through perseverance many people win success out of what seemed destined to be certain failure."

–Benjamin Disraeli

It will always take persistence to Live BIG!!!

5

LEARNING TO ADAPT

"The pessimist complains about the wind; the optimist expects it to change; the realist adjusts the sails."

–William Arthur Ward

One of the most important philosophies I developed through my own life experiences and years of study in personal development is the idea of the work-around. It is critical to find a work-around, or way to accomplish what you want in life, even if the path toward doing so isn't always obvious.

When I refer to a work-around, I'm talking about the idea that while the initial path or idea might appear out of reach or unattainable, there is a way to make it work. For example, my making a go of it in an industry dominated by people who speak eloquently for a living in front of large audiences when I was at a place in my life where I struggled to even talk on the phone. The idea on the surface appears unfeasible, but by following through with my idea and applying a series of work-arounds, I was able to act on the goal, which eventually grew into a successful business. My persistence and adaptability not only got me started in the personal development industry, but also got me to the point where I am now speaking to groups and organizations as part of my business. The roots of the idea of work-arounds started way back in grade school.

As a youth, my handwriting was nearly illegible. You had to be able to break code to decipher my writing. Well, I also was blessed to have an incredible teacher by the name of Ms. Presley. As much as anyone, she helped to instill in me a foundation of personal development I now teach to everyone I come into contact with through the speaking, writing, and coaching. That is—find a work-around. I learned how not to accept the challenges that come my way as the end result.

Here's how she did it. At a time when folks didn't rely on computers near as much as we do now in the classroom, she taught me how to type. That was my work-around. Simple, perhaps even obvious, and she did it.

That was a major step in my eventually formulating the idea that there's absolutely, positively always a work-around that can be applied for whatever personal success we as individuals strive for.

In fact, looking back I can see clearly now how the idea of the work-around helped me to overcome my disability in math. You see, while conventional wisdom might say we should be good in math if we hope to excel in business endeavors, my experience with the work-around told me that all I really needed to be good at was working a calculator or a spreadsheet. And of course, as I learned later on, I just needed to make the choice to work with folks who complemented my weaker areas and skills.

Let's apply the work-around to see firsthand how you can, with a bit of adjustment, make your way into an area that would bring you the same sense of fulfillment. While being a basketball player in the professional ranks might not be in "the plans" because of lack of height or physical talents out of your control, you could make your way into this field through any number of different avenues such as a coach or sports marketing and advertising. You could become an agent and represent athletes.

The sky is the limit when you allow yourself to remain open to all possibilities. You have to create for yourself an opportunity so you can take action and move in the direction you want to go.

LEARNING TO ADAPT TO LIFE CHANGES

In the example from my own life, I was at a time when I was experiencing quite a bit of anxiety, and the blocking tic left me struggling to even make a simple phone call. The idea of being a speaker who was paid to teach and present to groups and organizations was as foreign to me as any language other than my native English. Fortunately, rather than staying stuck in the obvious things I had going against me, I focused instead on the things I could do. I took the initiative to act on the idea of creating a Website where I could share the messages of the various personal development speakers and authors I had so enjoyed.

I reached out to people whose work I appreciated and shared my, admittedly limited, vision of wanting to develop a resource that others around the world could use in the pursuit of their own personal development. I adapted. I put persistence to work along with action, and, day by day, ended up taking that idea and developing it into a more formal business that ultimately went on to serve as the valuable resource that I had initially envisioned in my mind.

Long before I knew the details, I moved forward on the ideas as they showed up. The interesting thing is as you take action and see results begin to come together, more ideas come to mind, and the path begins to reveal itself. It's almost as though you have to prove yourself through your willingness to do what's asked of you, and as you do, you are given a new piece of the puzzle. As you place each piece of the puzzle that is given to you, you move closer toward your ultimate goal.

Another fascinating aspect of this journey is that the more you stay involved in the process, walking on the path toward building your dream, your knowledge grows exponentially to the point that what you once felt you lacked in vision or specifics, becomes clear and much more natural. It's as if you grow into the vision more each new day.

Our challenges, and perhaps equally as important the ways in which we figure out how to work within them, have the ability to completely transform our lives for the better, while breaking down the limiting beliefs that we all experience to some degree at different times in our lives.

Friend, a skill, once acquired, is yours to carry with you throughout your entire life. Even in the most extreme situations where you may no longer be able to practice your given skill set, you still have the working knowledge of that set of skills that are valuable. Obstacles can either be deterrents, or mountains to climb or walls to scale. The end result, the particular work-around you develop, may not resemble the approach you might have imagined to begin with, but the rewards that await you for having achieved your intended desire is just as sweet.

While it's important to set goals, it is also essential to give yourself the wiggle room necessary to adapt to changes that occur in life. As the saying goes, if you want to get somewhere you have to know where you're headed—and sometimes the path takes turns you weren't anticipating. It is true that you must be focused and persistent on the path toward achieving the goals you set, but also be willing to take any necessary steps that might reveal themselves along the way.

Success in any endeavor is rarely achieved by following a straight line, but that's not all bad. Life's changes and challenges can help keep things exciting, because it is through overcoming the challenges that we grow to the point where we can apply our acquired knowledge to any future endeavor.

The Solution Isn't Always Obvious

Often times we have a goal or a desire, but we think we lack the skills or training necessary to accomplish it. Not long ago I was speaking with a woman who was struggling with just such a situation in her life. She wanted to write a book. As we talked, it was apparent to me that she not only had the idea, she had the entire thing plotted out in her mind. I asked her why she hadn't already written it.

"Because I'm not a writer," she said. "I don't have the training necessary to do it. I don't know how to put my thoughts down on paper so that they flow like they do in my mind."

I could certainly understand that. So I asked, "Why do you think you have to be able to write to complete your book?"

She was naturally puzzled. "Seriously," I said, "it's obvious that you have the main ingredients all set. You just have to figure out the best way to make it happen. Here's what I suggest. First, let go of the areas in which you're lacking. Focus on what you have going for you. You've got the entire thing in your mind. That's huge! Second, let go of the part of your thinking that says there's a right way to do something. What matters in the case of the goal you've set is the final outcome—having your book completed. So why do you care how you accomplish it exactly?

"Here's an idea—get a tape recorder or digital recorder. Speak your entire book into it. If you feel more comfortable speaking parts of it into the recorder, do that. Once you have that done, have it transcribed. It's actually not that expensive. Alternatively, you could look for a writer or a journalism student who can help get your ideas written down in a readable format. The important thing isn't the specific approach you choose. What matters is that you take real action on your idea," I told her.

I could see her eyes light up. "It seems so obvious now. I never considered that I didn't have to spend the grueling hours I was sure it would take to write it myself," she said.

Isn't that interesting? All it took to help this woman get unstuck was to show her that there was more than one way to do what she wanted to accomplish. All too often we focus on the areas where we are lacking—where we need improvement. Whereas we would be that much farther along if we would simply work within the skills we have already developed and be willing to learn new ones along the way. There's a lot to be said about thinking outside the box.

And so it is with whatever dream you hold for yourself. Whatever it is that you want to achieve—you have to know deep down that even though the solution may not be obvious, the key to your achieving it is within you.

ACTION STEP

Think back to a time when you were faced with an unexpected change in life that made you doubt your direction, yourself, and others. Did you eventually learn from that time, are you still stuck in that time? Take a step today to use that experience as a building block to take you forward.

LIVE **BIG**: BELIEVING IN YOUR ABILITY

"I believe in my ability to make my dreams a reality. Though the path may wind at times, and I may not always feel as though I am making fast enough progress, I know without a doubt that I will achieve my heart's desire. Challenges are nothing but opportunities to teach me what is necessary to get to where I want to be. As I overcome whatever adversity is in front of me, I become better, stronger, and more prepared to meet with the eventual success that will be mine."

LIVE **BIG**:
ACHIEVING YOUR UTMOST POTENTIAL

"I was made for greatness. Each time I step out of my comfort zone, I experience growth in some way—personally or professionally. I was not meant to live my life as a static being, never experiencing change of any sort. I was born to spend each day being the best I can be—striving to unleash my utmost potential. When I move in the direction of my dreams, no matter how insurmountable they may seem in this moment, all sorts of people, life situations, and opportunities appear that move me forward, like a

snowball down a hill picking up speed to bring my dreams into reality. Through action, persistence, and a willingness to learn along the way, my goals and dreams are transformed into reality!"

"Things turn out best for the people who make the best of the way things turn out."

–Art Linkletter

Find a way to adapt to the curves and disappointments of life and you will have found yet another way to Live BIG!

6

MOTIVATION AND INSPIRATION

"People often say that motivation doesn't last. Well, neither does bathing—that's why we recommend it daily."

–Zig Ziglar

I'm often asked, "What's the best way to go about keeping my motivation for the task at hand?" That's an important question, and one that might be best answered by looking at the following example.

Consider a time you remember having felt a true sense of joy in your life. It's likely that it was centered on some experience or the thought of some event happening, right? That's why we can rarely or fully recapture that feeling of happiness or joy, to the extent we felt it originally, when we are reflecting. Motivation is a state of being just as happiness is a state of being. Motivation is less a destination, or a place to arrive at, than a feeling that one experiences in a given moment.

Each of us has our own inner motivators—things that when triggered inspire us to some greater action. We can be motivated by others, sources directly outside ourselves, or something inside ourselves—a memory or even a fear or past experience that we don't want to see repeated or played out in our lives.

In fact, we can go from feeling completely uninspired to being ready to take on the world! The change in how we view ourselves, and in particular our ability to achieve a thing, can shift in a moment. I've seen people's perspective shift during the course of one presentation, a coaching session, as well as from reading or listening to a book or audio program. Many different things are capable of inspiring us to action when needed.

Staying motivated has less to do with finding a way to remain in a constant state of inspiration, and more to do with realizing that you have the ability to shift from your current state, if it's not serving to move you forward, to one filled with motivation to achieve whatever your given endeavor happens to be.

The key to tapping into your inner motivation and inspiration can be found in a number of different ways. Let's touch on a few of them now. If you put these ideas into practice on a regular basis, I'm confident they will serve you well.

BUILD MOTIVATIONAL MUSCLES

The way you begin your day counts—and it counts BIG time! In fact, it can actually frame what we take notice of throughout any given day. Consider that for the most part we have a blank slate when we begin our day. The things you do upon waking up can be critical, they can play a much larger part in how your day plays out than you might have ever considered. If you proactively begin your day taking in something of a positive nature, it's going to help you develop a positive attitude. You are going to be more equipped to notice the good that is around you.

Schedule regular points during your day when you refill your mind with positive material. Starting your day out right is powerful, but it's equally as important that you "keep your cup full." With the abundance of resources from which you can access personal development materials these days, there's simply no excuse for you not to make it a regular part of your day. This is easy to do, but it's also easy not to do. Make the choice to develop this positive habit, and you'll be infinitely better for it!

Join or put together a group of people who share your understanding of the importance of having positive, inspiring people in their lives. A few such ideas might include joining a small group at your church or a place of worship. You could also seek, or if need be start, a group that meets to discuss the latest personal development or audio program that you all choose to read or listen to. If there is no such group in your area, look online or start one locally. Be proactive and get yourself around a peer group that can support and inspire you.

Consider that the leading experts in any given field or industry, if they're truly worth their salt, make the ongoing commitment to study their craft. No one attains and sustains the level of mastery without being plugged into an ongoing learning mode. That holds true for personal and professional goals.

If you want to keep your level of motivation at its peak, you need to regularly partake of sustenance whether in a book like this one, an audio program, or whatever you choose that can regularly unleash your inner inspiration. The choice is yours!

DON'T CLING SO TIGHTLY TO THE PAST

Your past doesn't have to define your future—as long as you make the commitment not to allow it to do so. The sooner you get to where you can move past life's shortcomings, the sooner you will be able to start taking advantage of the vast opportunities that life affords those who don't allow themselves to stay stuck in the past. It has been said that the past is in the past, the future we do not know yet, and the present is a gift we can give ourselves.

FINDING POINTS OF INSPIRATION

Sometimes you hear a song, watch a movie, or read a book that moves you to the point of inspiration. It immediately fills you with a renewed belief that you can achieve whatever goal it is you set for yourself. Finding these inspirational nuggets can be far and few between, but when we uncover them, we know we've got something special that we can look back on when we need to relive that same inspiring feeling.

I knew I'd found another motivational gem when I'd finished watching the movie *Cinderella Man*. This is the story of boxer, James Braddock, later nicknamed the Cinderella Man due to his inspiring upsets in the boxing ring. He begins his career as a laborer during the Great Depression. Like most people in his position during this time, Braddock and his family are struggling to put food on the table. The opportunity comes up for him to fight against a well-known boxer who most folks thought would knock

Braddock out quickly. Braddock wins and also earns some much needed money to help his family. The upsets continue and Braddock eventually finds himself in the ring against the world champion who is expected to destroy Braddock. Of course, Braddock upsets him as well, becomes the world champion, and brings comfort and success to his family.

I find myself going back to watch it often as it inspires me very much. Everyone needs a good motivational pick-me-up from time to time; and for me, this is just such a treat. My hope in sharing this with you is that you will be aware of inspiration points when you encounter them, knowing you can use them in the future to further fuel your own achievements. They show up all the time in obvious and not-so-obvious ways and places, but you have to stay on the lookout for them.

LAUGHTER, LIFE'S GREAT ELIXIR

Make a point to introduce a little laughter into your day. Much like taking a vitamin, it'll do wonders for promoting more joy and happiness in your life. Instead of just waiting to laugh, be proactive about it—do things that will actually cause you to smile more, or even burst out laughing. A few ideas include: Watch or listen to a comedy. Think back on a humorous event that makes you smile. Take a moment to experience a bit of laughter. Laughing has the power to change your current state or outlook.

Don't believe me? The next time you're feeling down, see for yourself how impossible it is to stay in a sad state when you're experiencing something that truly takes your mind off what's bothering you and makes you laugh. It might not be a permanent fix, but often all you need is relief in the current moment. And that's worth considering isn't it?

ACTION STEP

Make a deliberate effort to watch for signs of inspiration and to sustain your motivation. Write down five things, places, or people who have inspired you in the past. Write the reasons you were inspired and use that moment to recreate others.

LIVE **BIG:**
EXPERIENCING YOUR ACHIEVEMENTS

"It is important that I take the time to slow down enough to acknowledge the achievements that have come my way in life. I understand that because life can move quickly, and challenges may pop up when I least expect them, if I don't take time to stop and smell the roses along the way, I'm likely to feel overwhelmed. Positive experiences are always occurring—yet if I am not careful, they are often overshadowed by their negative or less desirable counterparts. It is up to me to slow down long enough to fully experience them. It is through fully experiencing the positive events and living my life to the max that I find fuel to move forward with the vigor necessary to uncover all the good that life has awaiting me."

LIVE **BIG:**
YOUR DAILY ACTIONS
CREATE YOUR RESULTS

"I have the power to create the life I want to live by the daily actions I take. Every day I am unleashing my greatness for the benefit of myself, my family, friends, loved ones, and everyone involved."

LIVE **BIG:**
RECONNECTING WITH
WHAT YOU WANT TO ACHIEVE

"I make a point to reconnect with the goals I have for myself—why I want to attain them, as well as all the benefits for having done so. Upon doing so, I have a renewed sense of my ability to achieve whatever I wish to accomplish. Through planning and a true commitment to work my plan, I am moving confidently in the direction of my greater vision."

"People who are unable to motivate themselves must be content with mediocrity, no matter how impressive their other talents."
                                    –Andrew Carnegie

Do what is necessary to stay motivated and inspired to Live BIG!

L E S S O N

7

ADVERSITY
AS A TEACHER

"Prosperity is a great teacher; adversity is a greater one."

–William Hazlitt

Prepare yourself for what might appear to be a bit of a bold statement. "Every adversity, every failure, every heart-ache carries with it the seed of an equal or greater benefit." Napoleon Hill, considered a legend in personal development and success thinking, offered that statement, and I believe he was right—and wrong. Before you think I've done the un-thinkable, doubted the wise words of Mr. Hill, in a public forum no less, please bear with me as I explain.

First, I will agree he was absolutely correct in that if people are honest with themselves and are willing to look objectively, they will see that their particular challenges actually made them stronger, even better prepared to meet with success in a given endeavor in the future.

That said, the challenge in the very statement from Mr. Hill is that in order to benefit from the lesson adversity has in store for us, we must be willing to first accept that there's a lesson in the first place. Confused? If so, don't worry, there's simply no easy way to state it; but if you stay with me for a moment longer, I promise to clarify my point.

It's up to us to choose to see the truth in his statement about adversity having in it a benefit, otherwise it's highly likely to go right over our heads. I believe this is very important. On the one hand, absolutely, every adversity has in it, whether we choose to see it or not, the opportunity for us to grow and in fact become better in some way for having experienced and overcome the given challenge. However, the second point is that unless we can hold onto the belief—especially when doing so is anything but easy—that along with every adversity we have the unique opportunity to grow as a result of working through whatever it is, then there is a very good chance that we're simply going to miss it all together. It's a bit of a catch 22 when you think about it, isn't it?

If you hold on to the idea and belief that your life challenges, no matter how difficult they may be at the time, can actually serve you in a positive way—somehow, someway—you find that you not only have the strength to continue, but you will come out on the other side better for having made it through.

By the same token, if you simply chalk up what's happening in your life as being "unlucky" or "life being unfair," or whatever other phrase you wish to use to describe your given situation, then your opportunity to grow is very likely going to fly right over your head.

Interesting isn't it?

My own life experience has shown me that adversity was, in fact, an opportunity to become better, more prepared in many cases for my eventual success. Adversity is something I've had my share of in life. As mentioned previously, I have Tourette Syndrome. The blocking tic that I've experienced as a symptom of Tourette's led to a phobia about phones. Not because I was afraid of the phone, but rather about people, clients especially, thinking I was a prank caller. When clients called me, it was embarrassing at times when they heard only dead air on the other end of the line. In short, I was unable to speak what I wanted to say. The best way to describe it is that I knew exactly what I wanted to say, the words were already in back of my throat, but try as I might, I just couldn't push them out. Here's how my adversity actually served me later on.

Prior to the blocking tic, I had been doing telephone sales in our family business. I was actually pretty good at what I did. Then when this particular challenge showed up in my life; I found myself feeling like many of the life skills I had developed to that point and taken for granted in some cases simply weren't available to me. After a while, I started a Website as a hobby type site—that eventually became GetMotivation.com.

After the number of visitors to that initial site increased, I decided to share my own thoughts and ideas on topics related to motivation and human potential. The only catch was, at that point in my life I was still dealing with the blocking tic.

The idea of sharing my message through traditional speaking or presentations seemed far-fetched to me at the time. It was very hard to articulate what I wanted to say.

Still, I knew I had a message that was worth sharing. The obvious (and only one it seemed at the time) solution appeared to be to write my thoughts as articles. While I didn't have any formal training as a writer or journalist, I opted to simply write as if I were speaking my thoughts. The key was that I made the choice to do the best with what I had at the time instead of waiting to have all the perfect writing and grammar skills before getting started. I committed to start, and learn and get better along the way.

While I had my share of critics, years later I can honestly say now that things have worked out for the best. What's most interesting and perhaps is a lesson I think you can learn and use from my life is this—when I began writing my thoughts, it was out of sheer necessity; however, years later, as I'm writing this, my verbal limitations are a thing of the past. I've been on many a stage, both in live appearances as well as teleseminars and other platforms, and each time I get better and better. Without a doubt, my ability to write and share my thoughts through articles and the written word has been one of the most important skills I have acquired. It allowed me to get around what might have been a career killer had I given up and not looked for a work-around. Then as time went on, I kept working on my speaking ability to the point where I am today.

Plus, writing gives me personal satisfaction and continues to present opportunities to me in my profession. What I viewed at the time as something I was doing out of necessity has become one of the most important pieces in the advancement of my profession. People from all around the world have become familiar with me and the work I do as a result of my writing. That, my friend, is the biggest proof I have to date that Mr. Napoleon Hill knew exactly what he was talking about when he said, "Every adversity, every failure, every heartache carries with it the seed of an equal or greater benefit."

Had I not always held on to the belief that I was as capable as anyone—no matter what challenges in life I happened to be facing—of achieving success in my life, I would have missed the incredible opportunity unfolding right in front of me.

UNCOVERING HIDDEN OPPORTUNITIES

In every adversity, you have the choice to remain paralyzed in non-action—neglecting to take the necessary steps that will put you on a corrective path. Or you can choose to take the proactive approach and ask the question, "What is the opportunity hidden in this challenge?"

Make no mistake, though hidden from plain sight, on the other side of every challenge is the opportunity to experience immense personal growth. Starting now, make the effort to view all challenges that come your way as hidden opportunities. This simple shift in mindset will make a tremendous difference in the number of accomplishments you experience throughout your life.

Whenever I speak to companies and organizations, immediately following my introduction—when someone recites all my personal and professional successes—I usually start by saying, "Funny, things never seemed to flow quite like that during the journey." Then I begin to share my personal story—the real meat and potatoes that led me to where I am at this point in my life.

I'd like to share with you a glimpse into my past in the hope that you can relate it to whatever challenges and adversities you may be working toward overcoming. Adversities are not your realities. You may find them to be right now, but you have all the power inside you to change your current reality just as I did. So my hope is that you will find courage in my story to move forward in pursuit of your own personal greatness.

Josh, the young years…

I was not considered a brilliant student. I could have applied myself more perhaps, but I still had some very real challenges. I was diagnosed with a learning disability in math in grade school, and not long after that I was diagnosed with Tourette's Syndrome. In my case, I was and am blessed that I have had a very mild case of Tourette's Syndrome. Yet, it was a challenge no matter the severity.

Josh the teenage years…

Aside from the obvious challenges I experienced while growing up; our family lived a fairly fortunate lifestyle. We were blessed with abundance in the form of monetary resources. My father was an excellent businessman. The exact year escapes me, but just prior to entering teenagerdom, our family experienced a very big lifestyle change. Through a business deal gone badly, all that my father (and our family) had achieved was gone. We found ourselves in the unfortunate place of having to start over. To emphasize how dire our circumstances, we had a car that had no reverse gear. You would be surprised how nearly impossible it is to find a parking place that you don't have to back out of. Through all this, my father never gave up. I believe much of my entrepreneurial spirit and perseverance is hereditary.

While it is true that the financial lifestyle change was a challenge for our family—one that I would not wish for anyone to ever have to experience—I now see clearly that it is responsible, as much as anything else in my life, for shaping me into the person I am today.

I say this because, first, but certainly not least, I was suddenly (for the better) in a place where I had only myself to give to anyone I wanted to become friends with. There were no fancy perks that came with being "Josh's friend."

I learned to accept people at face value and to be the best person I could be. I was banking on the idea that people attract the type of people by the type of person they are. Over time, I've come to realize that's an absolute truth in life. To this day, I am still in close contact with many of the friends I met during that time of personal adversity. To put it frankly, I don't think I'd be the same person I am now had it not been for what our family went through.

We started a new family business. Kudos to my father for understanding and teaching me through example that you can't always control what happens to you, but you can always control how you react to it! Times were still very lean, and we didn't meet with immediate financial success; but we were taking the actions necessary to head in the right direction.

So it was at 15 years of age I began working in the family business. As mentioned previously, I called on prospective clients on the phone to pre-screen and set the appointments for my father and the other commissioned salespeople who worked in the company.

Here I was at a point in my life where I thought I had things pretty well figured out. I had been studying personal and professional development; and with all this acquired knowledge and skill at my disposal, it appeared to me at the time that suddenly losing my ability to communicate was a major adversity. Fortunately, I didn't give up, I certainly could have done more, but I did the best with the resources

I thought I had at the time and continued making the best of things—or so I told myself.

As time moved on, an opportunity opened for me to move to Louisville, Kentucky. While I wasn't there all that long, it was an incredible time of personal growth for me. I was exposed to a BIGGER outlook on business in general. I met some incredibly talented people and learned how to expand my thinking. I began looking beyond what people had achieved from a point of awe, and instead began thinking that if they can do it, so can I.

Josh, the young man…

I relocated back to my hometown of Tuscaloosa, Alabama, and along the way I registered my first Website address, which was the first step in what I do now. I had no idea that tiniest action would lead me onto my current path. Life is like that though; if you follow your passion, you don't have to know all the details in advance. You do, though, have to take real action and be willing to give your dead level best to all you do. In doing so, the details present themselves and your eventual success always unfolds.

LIFE IS NOT AN END GAME

As you've read what I shared, I do hope that you use it as inspiration for facing whatever challenges you may find in your own life. Life is not an end game. It's not about getting there as much as it is about enjoying it—often times right where you are in the moment. Truly, it's about the journey.

ACTION STEP

Identify an adversity that you are experiencing right now. Clearly define it and then clearly write steps of a work-around that will free you from the challenge and move you forward.

LIVE **BIG:**
LEARNING AND GROWING
THROUGH ADVERSITY.

"Through adversity and life's challenges I am made stronger for having overcome and worked through each particular hardship. I remind myself that on the other side of every challenge before me, I have within me, though it may be deeply hidden, the necessary ingredients to overcome and thrive. Truly I grow, become better and more prepared for having learned to work through whatever it was that was standing in my way. It's absolutely true that the opportunities for growth often reveal themselves in the darkest hours—not when things are easy. On the other side of every challenge is a new skill set that will move me ever closer toward the rewards that life has in store for me."

LIVE **BIG:**
KEEPING PERSPECTIVE

"I am careful to keep things in perspective. I take time during the day to recount my achievements, the progress I've made along the way to this point in my life. When I feel overwhelmed, I remind myself that the journey is often as important as the actual arrival. If it were not for the journey, the feeling of achievement associated with the goal wouldn't be nearly as sweet—nor as likely to be appreciated."

LIVE **BIG:**
ONGOING IMPROVEMENT

"Today and every day I am making a commitment to improve in some area of my life—either personally

or professionally. Each day offers the chance to grow, provided I am willing to dig in and put forth the effort to do so. The skills I develop now will pay great dividends as I move forward in the pursuit of my endeavors—whatever undertakings I may choose. Greatness is a part of who I am—this I believe with all my heart—through a combination of belief, followed by a commitment to action, I am heading on the right path that leads to my attaining my own personal definition of success. Of this I am certain!"

Adversity is like a strong wind. It tears away from us all but the things that cannot be torn, so that we see ourselves as we really are.
—Arthur Golden, *Memoirs of a Geisha*

As difficult as it may be, when adversity comes your way, look for the opportunity throughout the struggle and you will achieve personal growth and find the strength to Live BIG!

8

THE POWER OF ENCOURAGEMENT

"I consider my ability to arouse enthusiasm among men the greatest asset I possess. The way to develop the best that is in a man is by appreciation and encouragement."

–Charles Schwab

There's a saying that goes, "If you wish to receive more of life's rewards, create more value for theirs."

How do we go about creating value for others? Giving value can and does come in many forms. It can range from the referral that leads to a new source of business, all the way to the person who shares a smile with another, which in turn helps that person start the day on a positive note.

One of the simplest ways I know to make a positive impact is to adopt the role of people builder and encourager.

If you look for opportunities to point out the good in those around you, you will notice that others are not only more attracted to you, but in many cases BIGGER and better opportunities are as well.

> *"Be ever on the lookout for opportunities to teach others how to better their lot in life. It will amaze you how opportunities present themselves when you are viewed in the light of being a person who genuinely cares for and wants to see others succeed at their maximum capacity."*

–Josh Hinds

The simple fact that so few people practice the art of proactive encouragement puts those who make it a regular part of their routine in an enviable place. In a world where more often than not others are more interested in bringing others down to make themselves look better, those who build others up are a valuable asset to have around. Be that person, and you will reap more of the rich rewards that go along with doing so.

YOUR GOOD DEEDS RETURN TO YOU

What you put out in the world will inevitably make its way back to you. I'm the first to admit that when we are experiencing particularly hard times this appears to be the farthest thing from the truth. People, as a general rule, like to associate with, and when they're in a position to do so, work with, and hire those people who have an upbeat and positive attitude.

As you move through your day today, keep the following saying in mind, "Life's like a boomerang, the more good you throw out, the more you receive in return." To prove the truth in the ideas shared, carry a journal with you and keep track of how many times your "good deeds" make their way back to you in the course of a month or two. Don't go into this exercise looking to prove it wrong; or more than likely, that's precisely what you will end up doing.

Remember, more often than not, we get exactly what we focus on, whether that's a good thing or not depends at least to some degree on what we go looking for and take notice of in life.

THE MULTIPLYING POWER OF ENCOURAGEMENT

Of all the gifts you possess, truly one of the greatest is the ability to build up and help another person to do the best they can. An interesting thing happens when you give this special gift—much the same way a magnet works, you begin to pull into your life people, opportunities, and life experiences of positive natures.

To better understand this, consider the wise words, "You reap what you sow." What you put out to the world makes its way back to you. My friend, if you concede that there's truth in that statement; wouldn't it make sense to be proactive when it comes to looking for ways to encourage others? I think so!

Look at your life as though you are an artist with the ability to paint on your canvas a magnificent masterpiece. While this in itself is incredible, consider that you also have the added advantage of beginning a new work of art at will.

"Each new day is an opportunity to leave behind our shortcomings, and erase any missed opportunities. While it's true we are given a clean canvas to paint on it any picture of success we wish, we must believe this to be a

fact, and pursue each new day as though it is absolutely true."

–Josh Hinds

In this moment, you may find yourself on a path that doesn't serve you well. You can choose to correct your course. You have the ability to succeed at whatever you desire. Let go of the broken idea that it has to happen overnight in order to be deemed a success. With your brush in hand, start painting your life's masterpiece. You were made for greatness—believe it and live your life with an outlook of exploration and a willingness to let your gifts and talents flow.

THE UNSEEN BENEFITS OF DOING GOOD

Every day brings with it the opportunity to share a kind act with another. Yet, if we're honest with ourselves we can all recount a time when we have neglected to do so. With life moving so fast and all the demands it can place on us, it is no wonder we end up forgetting to pass out those kind gestures from time to time. Unfortunately, if we neglect to do so, we also miss out on the many benefits afforded to those who take the time to be kind to others. Not the least of which is the unique feeling of happiness and fulfillment within.

As you give, so you receive. You put yourself into a mode that allows you to better receive in kind what you have given. I don't claim to fully understand how it works, but I've seen it come to pass enough to know there's truth in it. I imagine you've seen it happen that way too, right?

When I was running my websites such as GetMotivation.com and others, I was sharing the work of people in the personal development industry. I was doing it because I enjoyed the content, but it also helped them in getting more exposure especially as my site continued to gain more traffic. When I began getting into the industry by writing and sharing my story, those same people, now friends, invited me to speak at their conferences and events that they were promoting. I never had some hidden motive of gaining these opportunities by sharing these people's work on my websites, but the opportunities came regardless.

There is something very empowering about taking the focus off yourself, if even for just a moment, and placing it on another strictly with the intention of making them feel good or empowering them. Think back to a time when someone gave you an encouraging word.

Consider also how it made you feel when you passed along that encouraging word to another. It made you light up just a bit even though you weren't the one on the receiving end, didn't it?

That's the essence of what I'm suggesting. Throughout your day, make a conscious effort to give deserving praise. If you make the choice to do so, you can transform the place you work and live. You can transform the interactions you have with those in your life—both personally and professionally. It's not magic, rather it comes to pass over time, sometimes slow, and other times they appear to pass in the blink of an eye.

CREATE YOUR OWN LUCK

I find it particularly disheartening when I hear someone refer to a person's success and achievements as simply luck. Or even worse...dumb luck. The word luck implies that the person had very little to do with the positive outcome she or he is currently enjoying. In fact, it even conjures up the idea that if someone is enjoying success, it could have easily been the result of going to the local store, purchasing a lottery ticket, and hoping for the best. The reality is that luck has little if anything to do with becoming successful. There are countless examples where the ingredients of being action-oriented and persistent had much more to do with the attainment and rewards of success than luck or happenchance.

Rather than use a word such as lucky, why don't we instead celebrate the fact that the person worked hard, put forth the ample effort, and is being rewarded for all that went into getting that person to where he or she is now.

The next time you hear someone calling a person's achievement lucky, I hope you will do both yourself and the other person a BIG favor and disagree wholeheartedly. Point out to the person all of the effort that the person most probably went through that brought success.

It's a simple shift in the way we choose to view things, but it is a shift that gives us power and the wisdom to know that we are as capable as anyone when it comes to reaching our dreams and desires.

Every day is an adventure. One in which we can write a storyline filled with new life experiences, positive relationships, and newfound success. Or it can be one in which we see little joy and sit back believing that success is something that is reserved for only the lucky few.

ENCOURAGE AND INSPIRE OTHERS

Make the choice to reach out to the person who appears to be alone—you might make a new friend or trusted colleague. At the least, you'll benefit from the act of doing a kindness for another.

Reach out to someone who might be struggling or looking for guidance. Offer to mentor that person. You have unique talents, gifts, and experiences that would benefit others who might be just beginning on the path you've been effectively navigating for years. You can be a hero to another person.

Your encouragement, given at just the right moment has the ability to propel you to near super hero status in the eyes of another. Therefore, don't be stingy with it; look for ways to inspire others to be the best they can be.

ACTION STEP

Today, find someone to encourage and inspire to reach his or her full potential.

LIVE BIG:
WHEN YOU BUILD OTHERS, YOU BUILD YOURSELF

"Today I will seek out someone and encourage them. I will find and acknowledge someone who is deserving. In doing so, I will not only be building the other person up, I will be building myself as well. It is impossible to build up and encourage another without experiencing the good feelings at least to some degree myself. Life will send back to me whatever I put out to the world. Therefore I strive always to put out and share things of a positive nature."

LIVE BIG:
ASKING YIELDS RESULTS

"Each day I will work to increase the likelihood that whatever I ask for will be granted to me by simply making a point to help others get what they want or are looking for. In order to do this, I will spend more time helping those with whom I come into contact. Whether clients, prospects, friends, or family, I will remember to ask the simple question, 'What can I do to help you?' As I strive to help others, so will I begin

to see that others tend to naturally show up in my life to help me accomplish the goals and dreams I have set for myself. I keep in mind the saying, 'Life is like a boomerang, the more good I throw out, the more returns to me!'"

"Correction does much, but encouragement does more."

–Johann Wolfgang von Goethe

Along your way, encourage others to Live BIG!

LESSON

9

ACTION

Destiny is not a matter of chance; it is a matter of choice. It is not a thing to be waited for; it is a thing to be achieved.

–William Jennings Bryan

People often ask me how to get started in a particular business or endeavor they want to pursue. To put it simply, my advice is to get started. Begin at least to some degree, as quickly as possible—even if they don't have all the specifics figured out exactly right to begin with.

My rationale for this thinking is grounded in sound life experience. I have seen time and time again in not only my life but those of many others, that life has an amazing way of filling in the details or supplying the people and or resources when they're needed for the person who chooses not to let perfection get in the way of undertaking endeavors.

I'm not suggesting anyone fly totally blind. Certainly, make sure you have a basic idea of the direction you want to move in; but at the same time, accept that as you find yourself in the activity and moving in the direction you want to go, that signs will appear, provided you're open to seeing them, which will help steer you in the right direction.

GET OVER THE PART OF YOU THAT SAYS, "NO I CAN'T..."

Friend, when you get past the part of you trying to convince you of all the reasons why you can't do a thing and get on with the business of just doing it to the best of your ability, you will be ahead of the game. You must accept that trying, even if doing so appears to be out of your reach, *is more than half the battle.*

The very fact that you gave it your dead-level best is indeed a win in and of itself. Because you had the courage to begin and have the persistence to stick things out, you are part of the special group of people who takes on their self-imposed comfort zones and gets on with the business of unleashing their greatness—knowing that in doing so they are creating opportunities for themselves and those around them.

Embrace the idea that you tried, which makes you a winner—and anything beyond that is gravy. When you get to the point where you find as much joy and fulfillment in having given a thing your best, in that moment you will find that the result you were after all along comes to fruition.

ACTION FUELS ACHIEVEMENT

The best ideas and education in the world won't help you if you lack the willingness to apply the necessary action to get started and the persistence to see things through. Always make action and persistence your secret ingredients on your path to success.

I was reading a magazine recently when an article caught my eye. It mentioned that most people who exercised regularly, and as a result tended to be in the best shape, were those who didn't plan out when they would work out, but rather worked out regularly without giving much thought to specific days or times. At first I thought, *how on earth do these busy folks ever find the time to get their workouts in?*

After a bit of pondering, it became glaringly obvious that by taking this approach they weren't allowing themselves to fall victim to the part of us that overanalyzes things. You know the one I'm talking about. The part of us that says I don't have time to work out, I've got to get home in time to make dinner. I've got to stay late at the office. I've got to—insert whatever comes to mind here. No, they simply act on their initial impulse to work out, to get that bit of exercise they feel they need.

It's such a simple thought: just get up and do that set of push-ups or go for that walk or run instead of taking that time to schedule it. I couldn't help but think that if we apply this same approach to just about any of our goals, we would find ourselves getting more accomplished.

Consider how many goals and achievements you have lost simply because you waited for the "right time" to get started—and therefore never took the necessary action to get started in the first place.

Is there ever really a "perfect time" to set out in pursuit of your goals? I mean, really. Is a month from now, two weeks, or a day from now going to be any better than right now, at this very moment? Probably not. That's just the way life works.

Life is filled with any number of things that will shift and change and inevitably occupy our limited time if we don't first take the initiative to fill it with those things we want to take priority in our lives

Starting now, get into the mindset that time, or a lack thereof, won't stop you from working toward achieving those things that you want to see manifest in your life. Instead of looking for the right time to get started, just get going on them and allow yourself the wiggle room to move and adapt to any change that might be necessary to get you to where you want to be.

As the saying goes, "You don't have to get it right starting out, you just have to get started." Change is inevitable, and in some instances it is true that we can't control every single thing that happens to us. Even so, there are active steps we can take that will help guide us in the direction of those things we desire. Simply sitting still and idle is one sure way to keep yourself from realizing your dreams.

Dream BIG and feed your dreams with the necessary amount of action; as a result, you are sure to attain your own definition of success. Keep this thought in mind: Even the best laid goals are simply dreams until you add the fuel of action that gets you on the path toward achieving them.

ACTION TRUMPS PLANNING EVERY TIME

Lest the subtitle of this section leads you to think I'm totally discounting the role that planning plays in the overall success equation, I do want to point out that I'm not against planning. Rather, in most cases, it's the order in which most people set out on the path toward achieving their given endeavors that deserves reconsidering.

Most people follow a path similar to the one listed below when setting out in the direction of whatever worthwhile endeavor happens to be occupying their mind at the moment.

1. The initial idea comes to mind.

2. Start planning and thinking about ways to accomplish goal.

During the regular planning process, generally one of two things begins to happen:

A. They begin to believe that by following the plan they've formulated they have a good chance of reaching success. From there they move forward working their plan or...

B. Self-doubt begins to kick in and before they know it, they are swimming in all the reasons why whatever it was that what once held promise in their mind is now suddenly something that they couldn't possibly achieve. At this point, most folks can just about hang it up, unless they have someone supporting them or they have developed the mindset necessary to overcome this "stinking thinking" and concentrate more on option A.

READY, FIRE, AIM

Fortunately, there's another option to consider. No matter what conventional wisdom may tell us, there's always another way, even if it's not always obvious. Rather than taking the approach most folks choose to take, which is basically a *Ready, Aim, Fire* approach toward getting things done (achieving your intended goals and dreams), I suggest adopting the *Ready, Fire, Aim* approach.

The difference, you ask?

In the first example:

Ready= your initial decision or commitment to pursue something worthwhile.

Aim =   the planning phase of things.

Fire =   the action you take that ultimately becomes
the difference between whether or not you
get started.

On the surface, this first option is fine. In fact, it has been proven to work just fine for many people. Yet, I'm convinced the second option—Ready, Fire, Aim—works even better. Why?

Let's look at it like this: You make the commitment to pursue whatever it is you're committed to accomplishing. But rather than running the chance of letting loose that part of you that wants to convince you why you can't do something, you bypass it almost completely and lead with some real action. That is to say, you get real, honest to goodness buy-in on whatever it is you happen to be pursuing. You're in the game.

Of course, the last step is important too, because after we've gotten started by taking action, we take Aim—that is, we plan. To some this might sound silly, but think of it like this. Our planning is in alignment with the importance of making corrections. I'm sure you've heard someone say that the definition of insanity is doing the same thing over and over again and expecting different results.

That's why the system I'm suggesting is Ready, Fire, Aim—and not just Ready, Fire, Fire, Fire, Fire. Because even though taking action early on is a good thing, it is possible that the action we have chosen is, well—wrong. Of course, the same end result can happen to our friends who made the choice to go the Ready, Aim, Fire route.

WIGGLE ROOM AND WRONG TURNS

The BIG difference is that you and I—by making a point to lead with action, and at the same time giving ourselves the wiggle room to learn from any wrong turns we make—inevitably end up achieving in our given endeavors far more quickly than those who chose to take the more common Ready, Aim, Fire approach.

When we set out with a sincere willingness to follow a worthwhile goal and are truly willing to learn whatever is required of us in order to reach the pinnacle of success in our particular undertaking, then those necessary people, events, and skills will show up.

There's a saying I bet you've heard before, "When the student is ready, the teacher will appear." To the best of my thinking that is very much why Ready, Fire, Aim gets results. In virtually every one of life's adventures, the person who makes a choice to lead first with action, even if initially it's little more than a sincere willingness to take action and move forward, will be better off than their counterparts who choose to run the risk of getting stuck in the planning phase of things.

I want to make it very clear that I'm not saying that planning in and of itself is the problem; rather, it is the fact that most people either plan to the point that they never get started, or they allow the fear of actually doing what is necessary to get in the way. They would be that much better off had they simply made the decision to step out into the unknown and start sooner rather than later.

Consider the following quote, "The doing of a thing makes it so." Throughout your day, look for times when you can repeat that simple phrase and gain strength from it.

ACTION STEPS

Consider the following quote:

> *"No one ever attains very eminent success
> by simply doing what is required of him; it*

*is the amount and excellence of what is over
and above the required that determines the
greatness of ultimate distinction."*

–Charles Kendall Adams

I'd like to share a thought of my own along this same topic for you to consider as well:

*"The average person says 'that's not my
job'—while the leader transcends their job
description and inevitably reaps untold rewards for doing so."*

–Josh Hinds

Strive to be the person who goes above and beyond what's necessarily expected of you, and you will see more of life's rewards making their way into your life.

LIVE BIG:
THE IMPORTANCE OF
TAKING CONSISTENT ACTION

*"Through consistent and focused action, I can ac-
complish and excel in whatever it is that I want to
achieve. Yes, that's a bold statement, but very true!
The size or amount of action I take isn't nearly as
important as making sure the steps I'm taking are
putting me in the right direction. Through ongoing
review, I can ensure that I stay on the path leading me to where I want to be. Success in my given
endeavors is, therefore, a matter of moving forward
each and every day, in some way—big or small,
making directional changes as needed. And getting
back on track as soon as possible. I'm as capable as
anyone of living my dreams; and at this very moment, I am making them happen!"*

LIVE BIG:
GIVE YOUR BEST TO THE TASK AT HAND

"I will give my best to the task at hand. Someone is always watching how I handle even the most menial of tasks. There are no small tasks, only opportunities to learn what is necessary to handle larger, more meaningful things in the future. I will make it a point to pursue whatever is in front of me to the best of my ability—it's worth the effort, and always pays off!"

"Small deeds done are better than great deeds planned."

–Peter Marshall

Take Action and Live BIG!!

10

SELF-CONFIDENCE

"Who has confidence in himself will gain the confidence of others."

–Leib Lazarow

I think there is a sad tendency in most people to underestimate just how powerful they are—just how much greatness lies inside them waiting to get out.

The reality is if you knew just how special you were and how much greatness went into making you the unique person that you are, I'm convinced you'd immediately know that nothing can truly keep you from achieving what you want in life. When you recognize this truth and then believe it, you are on the verge of accomplishing great things in your life. After you believe it, friend, go for it. You know you can do it! The extent that you want to live out your dreams and accomplish your goals is limited only by your ambitions.

AMBITION

Ambition is not something reserved for only the lucky few. If you don't believe that, look closely at the lives of those who have succeeded in various undertakings and you'll notice that many high achievers come from low socioeconomic backgrounds—Oprah Winfrey, Walt Disney, J.K. Rowling, Sam Walton, Jim Carrey, and Steve Jobs, just to name a few.

While there are those who would lead us to believe that success in a given endeavor is somehow out of our reach simply because of our background, race, education, or whatever, in reality nothing could be further from the truth. What is required of success is a person's willingness to acquire the needed skills, confidence in those skills, and the persistence to stay on task until his or her dreams are realized.

Greatness is indeed part of who you are—never forget that.

DEVELOPING YOUR ABILITIES

Contrary to popular opinion, life's rewards don't always go to the person with the most "natural talent," the best looking, or the lucky few. No matter what you may believe, the truth is everyone has a shot at getting ahead provided they are willing to do what is required of them to get to where they want to be.

The reason I can make this claim is because I have seen time and time again, where people from varying backgrounds, both with and without financial means, who have set out on a plan they deemed to be worthwhile, have moved forward on their given journey and seen it through to successful completion.

Without a doubt, one of the most important qualities you can develop is to adopt the belief that if one person is capable of something, then you are too—provided you're willing to remain persistent, adjust and adapt as your particular plan requires, and, of course, learn whatever skills happen to be asked of you. Self-confidence is the key here—you first have to believe that you can do what is asked of you.

You may have read this chronological list of Abraham Lincoln's life, but it is worth taking another look at it—a serious look—then gauge your willingness to adapt and develop your pathway to success. By his life and struggles, you can learn that success comes from having the confidence to keep trying no matter how many obstacles come up along the way. You must have the confidence to continue down that path to greatness.

1809 Born February 12.

1816 Abraham Lincoln's family was forced out of their home; he worked to support his family.

1818 His mother passed away.

1828 His sister died.

1831 A business venture failed.

1832 He ran for the state legislature. He lost. In the same year, he also lost his job. He decided to go to law school but wasn't accepted.

1833 Abraham Lincoln borrowed money from a friend to start a business. By the end of the year, he was bankrupt.

1834 He ran for state legislature again. He won.

1835	He was engaged to be married. His fiancée died; he was grief stricken.
1836	He had a total nervous breakdown and was bedridden for six months.
1836	Abraham Lincoln sought the speaker of the state legislature position. He was defeated.
1840	He sought to become elector. He was defeated.
1842	Married Mary Todd. They had four boys, three died.
1843	He ran for Congress. He lost.
1846	Abraham Lincoln ran for Congress again. He won.
1848	He ran for re-election to Congress. He lost.
1849	He sought the job of land officer in his home state. He didn't get the job.
1850	His son, Edward, died.
1854	He ran for the Senate of the United States. He lost.
1856	He sought the vice presidential nomination at a national convention. He lost.
1858	He ran for the Senate again. He lost again.
1860	Abraham Lincoln elected President of the United States

It's less about things being easy, and more about your willingness to adapt, develop your God-given talents to the best of your ability, and to be persistent. If you do that, you will inevitably amaze yourself with what you are capable of accomplishing.

My friend, life is a journey, but to fully see it, you must choose to experience it. Just because it's dull or unfulfilling in your mind doesn't make it so. The fact that others are living in the moment proves that life can be lived fully, but it begins within you to make it so through your actions.

Hold Tight to Your Integrity

While I might concede that the spoils of life don't always go to the most deserving, I hold true to the belief that without a doubt the spoils are always more enjoyed when the person has lived a life of integrity and didn't sell out the things valued most.

I have known successful men and women who have gone from the top to the bottom, and back to the top again, and a common thread among most of them is that they always held tight to their integrity.

I advise that you always make the effort to remain the person who never looks down on another, no matter in what place in life you may currently find yourself. If you are in an enviable place, be thankful, but don't live in a way as though you are above anyone else. Life often rewards those who remain humble no matter what success they acquire.

On Being a Born Leader

"Leaders are born, not made," right? Do you believe that? I don't believe it and here are three reasons why:

1. Look around you. Look at the military, businesses, schools, and other organizations. People are hired and recruited because management believes they can be leaders and make a difference. They say, in effect, "Join us. Listen to us. Practice what we teach…and we will help you make a difference with us." They look for and find difference makers.

2. Look at the people you know. I'll make you a bet. I'll bet you know some folks who have become leaders, people who influence others and make a difference in the world have done so using time-honored principles: good, hard study and applying what they have learned.

3. Look at me. Yep, you read that right. You may not know me very well, but I do, I'll tell you this: If you were one of those proverbial "flies on the wall" who was there throughout the various stages of my life, you would have noticed a few things. I didn't *act* much like a born leader. I didn't even *look* much like a born leader. I didn't accomplish a lot of born leader stuff.

But I did do this: I took a good, hard look at certain types of people—the "big guys" and the "little guys" who stand out above the crowd in terms of their impact. I looked. I learned. I acted. Did you get that? One more time: I found the right people, and then I looked. I learned. I acted.

Most folks don't think of themselves as a born leader. Chances are you don't. But you can become a person who positively impacts the lives of all kinds of people in all kinds of ways. You can. *You really can*. And if Josh Hinds can, *you* can. Caution ahead: Don't expect too much too soon. Don't expect a free ride with no obstacles.

But above all: Don't sell yourself short. Don't give up on your dreams. Don't stop believing in your potential. And don't quit looking, learning, and taking consistent actions in the right direction.

ACTION STEP

Develop the habit of reading the "success stories" of other people. As you read them, pay special attention to the challenges and adversities that often show up. Look for similarities; notice how they, like you perhaps, have challenges and adversities to work through and overcome. Take what you learn and use it as a source of strength as you move forward in the pursuit of your worthwhile endeavors. Develop self-confidence and move forward with assurance of your direction and eventual success.

LIVE BIG:
BELIEVE IN YOUR ABILITIES

"I believe wholeheartedly in my ability to achieve whatever I set my sights upon. If others can accomplish the goals they set, then so can I. Each day I take the time to review my written goals. I keep them nearby so they're never far from reach. I am moving confidently in the direction of my desired outcome. Each day I move further along the path to unlocking my full potential. I selflessly share my own unique talents for the good and benefit of everyone involved."

LIVE BIG:
DEVELOPING THE SKILLS TO SUCCEED

"I have inside me the ability to acquire whatever skills are necessary to achieve the goals I set for myself. Through ongoing effort, I am bringing into my reality the people and skills needed to achieve my own definition of success—for the good of all concerned."

"Don't wait until everything is just right. It will never be perfect. There will always be challenges, obstacles and less than perfect conditions. So what. Get started now. With

each step you take, you will grow stronger and stronger, more and more skilled, more and more self-confident and more and more successful."

–Mark Victor Hansen

Learn, grow, and be confident that you have what it takes to Live Big!

11

GRATITUDE

*"Develop an attitude of gratitude, and give
thanks for everything that happens to you,
knowing that every step forward is a step toward achieving something bigger and better
than your current situation."*

−Brian Tracy

*Gratitude is a source of fuel to move you forward during
the difficult times.* Gratitude is a feeling of thankfulness and
appreciation. While that definition is a good start, I think
gratitude is so much more than that. Particularly when we
begin to explore all the different ways it can serve us.

Something magical happens when we take the time to
recount all the things we have to be thankful for in our lives.
The past, present, and even the hopes we have for the future.

First, a sense of gratitude allows us to reconnect with our past achievements. These memories can serve as powerful reminders that in spite of whatever doubts we may have about our abilities in the present moment, we are capable of reaching whatever destination we desire for ourselves. We can change our circumstances and lot in life to a more desirable state.

FUEL FOR YOUR SUCCESS JOURNEY

Looking back on and reconnecting with positive experiences and past achievements is a particularly powerful way to go about providing fuel for your current goals and dreams. If you accept these ideas to be true, then what is the best way to go about expressing gratitude in your day-to-day life? The answer, to put it bluntly, is to express it however it feels most right to you!

Since I don't know what that is in your unique situation, I'll have to settle on showing you some of the ways I go about it on a daily basis.

1. *Upon waking, I begin running through my mind various things, people, places for which I'm thankful.* Inevitably one thing, person, or event will lead to another. This is a laid back experience; all the while I'm trying to remain in the moment, but not forcing it. If I find my mind moving on to other thoughts or ideas, I'll gently bring myself back to this simple exercise. When I do this, almost immediately I can see my current emotional state perk up a bit—and I take on a more positive outlook. I find it a simple, yet highly effective way to start my day off on the right foot. I believe you will as well!

2. *Throughout the day I like to write down my "daily wins."* These aren't always monumental

achievements. To the outside observer, many of the accomplishments that I record might appear downright mundane. The point of the exercise is to remind myself of something I discovered a long time ago: to meet with success in virtually any endeavor requires a lot of little accomplishments along the way.

When I'm speaking to groups, I'll often say that the path to success is paved with more than its share of boring moments. When someone looks back on a worthwhile accomplishment, there's rarely one particular event to which the person can credit being totally responsible for reaching the pinnacle of success. Rather, if we're honest with ourselves, we would likely have to agree that it's a matter of doing those required tasks, day in and day out which allowed us to reach our goals. The journey, you see, takes many forms. Certainly at times things are fast-paced and exciting; but at others times, persistence and stick-to-it-ness are required.

If you're not already tracking your day to day achievements, I'd strongly encourage you to get started. This way you will have a trail to look back on and read over when you aren't feeling quite as plugged into your dream as you wish you were. You have proof positive that you're making progress right in front of you. Then, at the end of each day as you look through your list of wins, you can take a moment to be grateful.

3. *Take a walk and recite out loud all the things, people, and experiences for which you are grateful.* I have to give credit to my colleague,

friend, fellow speaker, and author Jon Gordon for this idea. While I had actually been doing this for a long time prior to first hearing Jon mention it, he deserves credit for putting the name "Gratitude Walk" to it. This helped to validate my belief that it was a worthwhile thing to do (and that no matter what my neighbors who happen to see me talking to myself might think, I'm not actually nuts for doing so).

These may sound like simple ideas, but I challenge you to give all three a try. If you will do so, I believe that in relatively short order, you will find them to be welcome additions to your daily routine.

As I've illustrated, expressing gratitude is a powerful thing. It can change your state of mind from one in which you may be feeling doubt toward one of hope, and a sense of being filled with encouragement. It can put you in a mode to accept the good that surrounds you, while acting as a sort of shield from the part of your mind that wants to seek out the negatives in your life. Give the ideas a try. If you have other ideas that work for you, please share them with me!

The Keys to Staying Happy, Fulfilled, and on Target

THE KEYS TO STAYING HAPPY, FULFILLED, AND ON TARGET ARE:

- Defining what success means to you.
- Setting goals.
- Visualizing future achievements.
- Persistence.
- Adapting.
- Motivation and inspiration.
- Adversity.
- Encouraging yourself and others.
- Taking action.

- Believing in yourself and your capabilities.
- Being grateful.

You will notice that these keys are the topics discussed in the first 11 chapters, or lessons, of this book. Each key unlocks doors of opportunity that you may have never even considered. Open wide your mind and the doors to absorb a higher level of living, learning, and dreaming. You have unlimited resources at your fingertips, and your mind is capable of so much more than imagined. Reach out toward your BIG life today!

THE PARADOX OF GIVING AND RECEIVING

Wouldn't it appear that giving, without regard to any positive outcome in return would be about the furthest thing from a conduit for receiving there is? Yet time and time again, if we really think about it, we can see examples where the act of first giving, whether of our time or material assets, inevitably leads to our receiving something of equal or greater value in return. We don't give to receive, yet that is of no consequence. Receive we do just the same. Consider the following examples to further illustrate what I'm suggesting:

The salespeople who give great service, putting their customers' needs squarely above their own, receive compensation both in the form of profit or commission, but also receive positive word-of-mouth comments, and in many cases, referrals from those they serve.

Consider the parents who give of themselves in the form of unconditional love, time, and finances to raise their children. They receive the amazing gift of one day having raised adults, who go into the world spreading the incredible legacy that their parents first planted in their children so many years before.

Friend, if you take the time to look for them, you'll see that there are countless examples of where our willingness to first give of ourselves and or resources in some way leads to receiving, in often unexpected and exciting ways. Be grateful for these times.

As you move through your days and weeks, consider ways you can share kind acts with others. More importantly, be grateful for these opportunities, and act on the ideas that come to mind. Watch as the seeds of kindness you plant blossom and inevitably make their way back to you!

Then, just for today, choose to slow down just a bit. Choose to watch a sunset—or if you're an early riser, a sunrise. Decide that during this time you will block out any apprehension you might be feeling about what's going on in your life, just long enough to fully be in the moment, and grateful for what you do have.

ACTION STEP

Buy a small notebook that fits in your pocket, purse, or briefcase. Use it to write down your "wins" and all the things, people, places, experiences, etc. for which you are grateful. Write down ways you can show kindness to others and commit to doing something kind for someone once a day.

LIVE BIG:
MAKING THE MOST OF TODAY

"Today I will make the most of this day. I will do the same tomorrow, and the day after. In doing so, I know that I will experience the positive outcome I hope for. I can overcome whatever life challenges I may face. Each day I find comfort in knowing that the right actions I am taking are indeed moving me on the path toward achievement in my particular endeavor. Every day I look for ways to do those

things that will move me closer to what I wish to achieve. Each time I do one of the tasks I've identified, I am making real progress. When I do the thing I am resisting, I give power to that part of me that propels me even further on my own personal success journey."

LIVE BIG:
BEING GRATEFUL

"Each morning before rising to start my day I think about the people, events, and things I have to be thankful for in my life—and I give thanks for those things. Doing this simple act starts my day on a positive path of appreciation, and it is a wonderful reminder that whatever challenges I may be facing in the moment, I do in fact have much to be grateful for. Happiness begins to take hold in the moment I take inventory of the good that surrounds me."

LIVE BIG:
TRACKING YOUR DAY-TO-DAY WINS!

"I take the time to write down my day-to-day wins. When I remind myself of past achievements and daily successes, it provides the necessary fuel to move me toward the goals and dreams I hold for myself. Often something as simple as reminding myself that I've faced challenges before is all I need to continue moving forward in the pursuit of my endeavors."

"Gratitude is a vaccine, an antitoxin, and an antiseptic"

–John Henry Jowett

Take time to be grateful along your journey to Live BIG!

12

THE POWER
OF KINDNESS

*"What we give inevitably makes its way
back to us. Whether those things are good,
bad, negative, or positive—they all make
their way back to us over time."*

–Josh Hinds

What got me itching to write about this topic of being kind was a movie I watched recently called *Pay It Forward*. If you haven't seen it, I highly recommend it. The
basic premise, at least what I get from it every time I see
it, is that by doing acts of kindness for others, even people
we don't know, we have within us the power make a BIG
impact and even change the world around us for the better.
Pay it forward instead of paying it back thereby spreading

the kindness and goodwill to more people. This may seem a little too good to be true, right?

There was a point in my life where I might have said the same thing. At times when things happen that don't appear to make sense to me, I admit it can be easy to discount acts of kindness as well. However, just about the time I find myself doubting the power of kindness, I am the receiver of someone's random act. Perhaps you can relate to this occurrence?

I'm reminded of one of my favorite quotes by Zig Ziglar every time I give serious thought to the idea behind random acts of kindness. He says, "You can have everything in life you want, if you help enough other people get what they want."

ACTS OF KINDNESS BLOSSOM

One could make the case that there is a difference between Zig Ziglar's quote and the motivation behind random acts of kindness. After all, aren't the acts of kindness supposed to be completely random? That is, we do them without any direct expectation in return? This is true. I would, however, take it a step further and say that Zig's quote may have a deeper interpretation.

How so, you ask?

Well, the way I see it, Mr. Ziglar is suggesting we actually make the idea behind the quote a lifestyle. A lifestyle in the sense that everything we do is built upon service to others. Not serving others only if we see a direct or immediate benefit. That is the point at which I believe both ideas meet. In both random acts of kindness and choosing to lead a life built on serving others, we put ourselves into a natural state where the things we send out, give freely to others, naturally come back to us in some form or another.

In both instances, the point is not that we benefit directly, or selfishly, but so that others will receive a benefit. The ironic aspect: it's through our giving without expectation that we are rewarded in ways often beyond what makes logical sense. You can refer to this as the law of reciprocity, which is perhaps best explained by the idea that we are paid back for the good we do.

The flip side is also true. We are also repaid for the negative and bad things that we put out.

To further illustrate the point, I share the following story with you. You may have heard or read it previously, but it is worth the repeat.

A man was walking on the beach one day when he came across a place where a number of starfish had been washed upon the shore. He noticed a young boy who was feverishly running back and forth trying to put the starfish back into the ocean. After watching the young fellow for a while, the man said to him, "Don't you know you can't possibly save them all? Why are you wasting your time like this?" After the boy put another starfish back into the ocean, he replied, "It made a difference to that one."

Customer Service Skills — Kindness in Action

Instead of seeing someone who takes the time to complain about a product or service you've rendered as an annoyance, try to reframe it for what it really is — an opportunity to grow, learn, and ultimately become better for the experience. Remember, it's been said many times that we actually grow more by going through life's challenges, than during those times when it's smooth sailing.

When a person takes the time to share what they think is wrong, be thankful, because so few people actually do. Instead, most people go silently into the marketplace sharing their negative experience with others rather than the ones who could solve the problem.

For this reason alone, isn't it better to correct any disagreements early on? If the other person asks for a refund, strive to give it without hesitation or making it difficult on them.

In virtually every case, you will find that you're always better off when the other person leaves the experience feeling good about it even if you weren't able to deliver on what you both originally agreed upon.

In the short-term, you may feel that you've lost; but in reality, you have built trust and paved the path for the other person to do business with you at another time. Not to mention you will be surprised by how many people will actually sing your praises to others as they share what a rare customer service experience they had, "with the person who really wanted to make sure I left the transaction happy." So few people take this kindness approach that when you do, you will put yourself at a distinct advantage in the marketplace.

If you can develop the ability to render this level of service with a smile, you will distinguish yourself in a positive light. The rewards for this attitude are well worth the effort it takes.

When you build trust through your actions, you strengthen your character. Your character determines your influence. Your influence determines the level of success you will attain—be it personally or professionally.

ACTION STEPS

Consider sharing your smile with another person. Yep, I'll admit this sounds simple, but you can't imagine what a positive impact a friendly smile can have on another person, until you're the person receiving one.

When going through a toll booth with a fixed amount, consider paying for the next person in line. The other person doesn't even know you did it. Remember, we're talking about random acts of kindness. First, the person will be completely surprised. And since you're not doing it in front of the person, the person won't feel obligated or uncomfortable. This sort of random act of kindness also has the power of being carried on several people down the line.

Send a card or an email to someone. Something as simple as receiving an unexpected card or email can make all the difference in the world to someone who may be feeling lonely or under the weather. You don't have to write a novel. A short and to the point message can be incredibly powerful. Simply let them know you wanted to stop what you were doing to write them and let them know you appreciated them, and why.

Consider leaving positive and encouraging quotes to people who sit down in the seat (or at the table) you just left. The idea here is to be anonymous. Don't leave your name. Simply share a positive thought or quote. You might even consider making 3x5 cards with positive quotes and sayings on them that you can leave at random places throughout your day. Again, the idea is to be totally anonymous.

While driving and arriving at a stop sign at the same time as another person, motion for the other person to go ahead.

If in a long line at the bank, grocery store, or convenience store, let the person behind you go ahead of you.

Hold the door for the person behind you when entering a mall or department store.

Have your change or check ready for the cashier so you don't hold up the line behind you when at the check-out.

Bake some cookies and deliver them to a neighbor.

Think about how these acts might have a positive impact on you. Would they make you smile? If you were at a point in your day where things weren't quite up to par, might they be just the ticket to give you that needed positive jump-start? See, that's the point. Random acts of kindness benefit the giver and the receiver.

These are just a few ideas that you might want to consider. I hope you make up some of your own ideas as well and begin as soon as possible the action of showing good to others. Everyone benefits: the other person, the people they come into contact with, and ultimately you.

LIVE **BIG**:
MAKING SURE EVERYONE WINS

"Contrary to what some may say, in order for me to experience success in a given endeavor, there doesn't have to be a loser. In every undertaking, I strive to leave a trail of people who have shared in my success. When I place a strong importance on making sure that others have a positive experience from having worked with me, I find that I attract people into my life with the exact same outlook."

LIVE **BIG**:
BEING PREPARED

"Opportunities are all around me. In fact, they are always popping up even when I least expect them. Therefore, I make a point to always be prepared when the inevitable chance appears for me to shine at whatever undertaking I happen to be involved in. The opportunity to advance finds the person who has prepared and is ready for all that is involved in the particular event. I am fully prepared to step right

into whatever I hope to achieve, rather than taking the approach that I will learn what is needed should I be chosen."

"Kindnessisalanguagewhichthedeafcanhear and the blind can see"

–Mark Twain

Showing kindness to others is a staple characteristic of all those who Live BIG!

13

THE POWER
OF THOUGHTS

"Change your thoughts, and you change your world."

–Norman Vincent Peale

I'm often asked how I can stay so positive. Allow me to clear up some misconceptions you might have based on that statement. I am not one of those folks who walk around with what is commonly referred to as a "career politician's smile" painted across my face. I believe in the power of a *genuine* smile, not fake happiness. No matter how much of an overall positive person I am, I still have my down times. I call it being human.

The fact that we are human ensures that we will all—from time to time--have down moments. The difference lies in how quickly we choose to get over those things that are holding us down or back, or making us feel less than our personal best. I believe that is a major key—being able to get past the down times in life as quickly as possible and getting back to being your best. Always be moving in a continuous improvement mode.

Remember, self-improvement is a hands-on project. That is to say that without ongoing implementation and attempting new ideas, try as we might, we aren't going to miraculously wake up one day changed people. No, we've got to apply those ideas and bits of advice we learn. Most importantly, it's how *you* can lead a more positive daily life. And it's not really all that complex, is it?

When you first wake up each morning, you have a fairly clean slate, a new canvas. In most cases, your day is fresh—neither overly negative nor positive. Importing positive thoughts (reading, listening, reciting, etc.) first thing in the morning and throughout your day can do wonders toward reprogramming your mind and the overall way you see your world.

Here's your homework for today. Ugh! I was never a great student, so even hearing that word gives me the shivers—maybe you too? Even so, like I said before, self-improvement is a hands-on project, so it's worth getting over it and embracing the view that you are a lifelong learner. I did, and I can tell you that I'm infinitely better for it, and I'm certain you will be as well. It really is just a shift in your thinking from "I'm not a good student" to "I enjoy learning for what it will make of me." Simple? Of course, and I'm living proof that simplicity is often all it takes.

So here's what I ask you to do:

Write the following quote on a 3x5 index card or on something you can keep handy and not lose it:

"People often say that motivation doesn't last. Well, neither does bathing—that's why we recommend it daily."

–Zig Ziglar

Read the quote several times a day. Also, choose to read something or listen to something of a positive nature at least three times a day, preferably, morning, noon, and evening. What would be even better is if you could immediately counter any and all negative experiences with something positive.

Given the events of most people's days, carving out time to read or listen isn't always feasible, but it can pay dividends and is worth attempting. The BIG thing to keep in mind is that no matter how great any idea or advice is, unless you choose to implement it and give it a fair shot to work its magic in your life, you're not going to get results.

"Remember, great ideas can be a dime a dozen. It's the ability to put forth the necessary action to get started on them, or put together a qualified team of people to execute the idea that separates the wheat from the chaff when it comes to achieving success in virtually any endeavor."

—Josh Hinds

You have to be part of your own success journey. If you want to see real, lasting change for the better in your life, you have got to be the BIGGEST part of the process.

Knowing that you can offset your negative feelings by introducing positive thoughts into your mind simply isn't enough. No. You have to actually do it! That means keeping a motivational book or tape handy to refer to when you need it. It might mean stopping what you're doing at the moment or even scheduling (and sticking to it) time to take in positive or motivational material.

Like dieting or exercising, developing a positive mental attitude is a choice. It requires nurturing. It's not always immediate, but if you work on it and cultivate it, you will see results. And those around you will as well.

Do You See the Positive Side of Things?

There are generally two ways of seeing things in life. We can choose to view life through negative or positive filters. Perhaps you've heard it referred to as seeing through rose colored glasses when things are viewed in a positive light. When I'm faced with situations in my life and I have the choice to assume the best or worst, I like to recite the following quote to myself—and to others: *"Until you're proven wrong, you might as well assume you will receive the best possible outcome."*

I think there's a lot of truth to the term self-fulfilling prophecy. This means that if people think of all the reasons things can't possibly work out for them, they end up giving power to the very things they don't want to happen. It is true that we tend to get what we focus on. That being the case, doesn't it stand to reason we would benefit from seeing things through a more optimistic lens?

I'd also add that I'm not saying that everything is going to work out for the best in every single instance. However, even in the worst of times we can choose how we respond to the things that happen to us. We can make the choice to do what is necessary to dig ourselves out of the place we are now—reminding ourselves that in time, if we refuse to give up and stay in the game, our life will turn for the better and we will see the positive results we desire.

THOUGHTS BECOME THINGS...
THEY REALLY DO!

As I'm writing this, I'm looking at my vision board. (If you're not familiar with a vision board, don't fret, I explain later.) On it are several things, goals I want to see manifest in my life. At the top it reads very simply: Vision Board — Thoughts Become Things.

I'm fully aware that some would read that heading and argue that just thinking of something is not enough to make it happen. To which I would concede that's partially true.

Notice I say only partially true, because we're not just talking about fleeting thoughts here. What I'm referring to is someone's dominant thoughts. Those thoughts that are so ingrained in our minds that we naturally take the necessary actions needed to see them through to the point at which they become reality. There is a BIG difference between a dominant thought and simply thinking you'd like to have something.

When it's a dominant thought, it sticks with you. Think of it like the difference between Super glue and the Elmer's glue you used in grade school. You are always asking yourself how you can go about making your particular endeavor a reality, and when you find that one plan of action doesn't work out as you'd hoped it would, you don't just quit. When something is a dominant thought, you understand that each attempt is simply part of the learning process from which you can grow — and by trying another approach you will get that much closer to what it is you truly desire.

Hopefully you will give me the benefit of the doubt and believe me when I say there's a lot of truth in the saying, "Thoughts become things."

Now here's the rub. Assuming that's true, that the thoughts and ideas we focus on most become real and tend to show up in our lives, it's worth pointing out that the saying doesn't discriminate. Listen up, because it's that important. Here's what I am saying, if you're focused on negative things, you're going to see negative results and events creep into your life. It is the same if you are focused on positive things or events. The reality is that it works both ways.

Here's an illustration to make my point. Recently I was having a conversation with someone who was telling me about their new manager. This person was just absolutely sure that the relationship between the two was going to be a disaster. This person had already made up her mind before the new manager had ever even appeared in the office for the first time. Well guess what? The first week was absolutely terrible! This person almost transferred to another department.

Fortunately, time was given, and low and behold, things weren't nearly so bad after all. Isn't it funny how life works like that? You see, this person was so absolutely sure it was going to be awful that those thoughts became a self-fulfilling prophecy. Quite simply, her thoughts became her reality.

I'm happy to report that the last time I talked to this person she told me she was surprised that it might actually end up being a good thing. Now she's seeing things through a positive lens, and guess what she's getting? You got it, more of what she's focused on.

Now I will say that in absolutely every instance this might not work out exactly as I've said. However, I think the quote by Zig Ziglar makes a terrific point regarding that. He said, "Positive thinking will let you do everything better than negative thinking will."

So assuming you concede that your dominant thoughts, either positive or negative, tend to become your reality, doesn't it make sense to think and take action on the things you want to see in your life, rather than those you don't? Remember, either way you're going to get something, so it might as well be of your choosing, don't you agree?

Now before you think I've broken my promise to cover vision boards, here's a quick overview. It is by no means exhaustive, but I think it's worth mentioning in case you're not familiar with them.

First, there is a number of ways to make your vision board as elaborate as you'd like. I won't say you have to include all the bells and whistles on yours for it to be effective. It's a personal preference.

The one I'm currently looking at is pretty blah—but it isn't the design or layout that's powerful, it's the thoughts and things that are written on it. It's a piece of cardboard on which I have written goals and pictures that represent the things I'd like to see transpire in my life.

When I focus on those things on my vision board, my mind can more easily go to work doing the things that drive me toward taking the necessary actions needed if I want to see those things become a reality.

Consider it a powerful reminder of what you want to achieve. Plus, like your success journal (hopefully you keep one), it can end up being quite an incredible source of personal validation as you're able to actually see the things on your vision board come to fruition in your life.

So that is what makes up a vision board. Again, nowhere near an exhaustive overview, but I think it gets the point across. It can be an incredibly effective tool to use in your personal journey toward achieving your goals.

Vision boards work because they help keep you plugged into the things you want to achieve. But like anything, you can't just keep your vision board hidden away where you never see it. Think of it as a billboard, but instead of advertising, you are putting thoughts about your important goals and dreams into your mind on an ongoing basis.

You Attract What You Focus On

What you allow yourself to focus on is what tends to transpire in your life. Therefore, the question you must continuously ask is, "Do I want more of this in my life?" If the answer is anything short of "YES!" then you need to shift your thinking to focus more on those things and experiences that you want to see occur in your life.

Knowing when our thoughts are no longer serving us helps to move us in the direction of the goals we have set for ourselves. It is an important part of getting back into alignment, back to the place of doing those ongoing actions required to see our dreams through to completion.

Take Command of Your Thoughts

Accomplishing the goals you set for yourself is largely a matter of consistently keeping the junk thoughts that pop up throughout the day to a minimum. You know the ones I'm talking about—those little voices that tell you all the reasons why you can't possibly pull off what you wish to accomplish.

If you can keep this rubbish thinking to a minimum, you will amaze yourself with the number of successes you can rack up in life.

Action Steps

Create your own vision board. Include pictures, or write something, anything that will represent what you want to achieve. In addition to the more traditional vision board mentioned you could play around with what I call a mini-vision board. Take some 3x5 index cards and basically do the exact same as you would with a vision board. The index cards approach will be a lot easier and convenient to carry with you than a traditional size vision board would be. Remember the old and true saying: out of sight, out of mind. Finally, whatever you do, do something. The more you keep the things you want firmly in mind—and sight— the better the odds you will give yourself to making them a reality in your life.

Live BIG:
Achieving the Outcome I Desire

"I guard my thoughts, making certain that to the best of my abilities I am ever focused on the positive outcomes I want to achieve in my life. I am equally aware of the importance that taking the necessary action plays in my acquiring the success I desire."

–Josh Hinds

Live BIG:
Like Attracts Like

"I am committed to being the type of person with whom others want to associate. Each day I practice being kind, being generous, helpful, and an encourager to all (even when there may appear to be no direct reason for doing so). As I develop the habit of doing these things, I notice more and more that these are the exact qualities that appear in the people I meet and associate with. I take the time to give thought to the old saying, "Like attracts like," and am reminded just how true it is."

LIVE BIG:
CREATING POSITIVE OUTCOMES

"I keep clearly in mind the saying, 'I can't always control what happens to me, but I can control the way I react to what happens.' When I make the decision to react in a positive way, I am putting myself in a position where I am likely to experience a positive outcome. When I choose to perform to the best of my ability, life has an interesting way of filling in the blanks—the bits and pieces I may not have seen originally. Starting today, I am committed to doing my absolute best in all my endeavors; by doing so, I am walking confidently along the path that is moving me ever closer to where I want to be."

"A man is but the product of his thoughts--what he thinks, he becomes."

–Mahatma Ghandi

Start thinking BIG and eventually you will Live BIG!

14

LEARNING
FROM OTHERS

"A man only learns in two ways, one by reading, and the other by association with smarter people."

–Will Rogers

Developing and cultivating strong mentor relationships and peer groups will move you forward in life. Learning from those who have successfully overcome trials and challenges launches you forward at an amazing speed. Rather than suffering through an experience by yourself, look for someone who has already found the solution for your dilemma.

"The people you interact with are the sum total of all the success you are likely to acquire in your life. Knowing that, is your

peer group moving you in the direction of your overall potential?"

—Josh Hinds

ENTREPRENEURIAL THINKING— AN ESSENTIAL SKILL SET

On my father's side of the family, we have several generations of entrepreneurs and small business people, including my great grandfather, my grandmother, one of my grandfathers, my father, two of his brothers, and then me. I'm certain I'm leaving others out, but it's not intentional, it's just that we have a lot of entrepreneurs in our family tree. A fact that I'm quite proud of, I might add. Suffice it to say I'm cut from the entrepreneurial cloth if ever there was one.

I mention these examples to make it abundantly clear that I'm a firm believer that everyone would do well to adopt and develop a strong entrepreneurial mindset. I also believe people put future generations at a strong advantage when they actively encourage and cultivate entrepreneurial skills in our children and young adults. These skills can take them far in life, and I think we do them a disservice by not requiring that they learn them at least to some degree.

Developing the entrepreneurial mindset doesn't necessarily require people to be entrepreneurs themselves. While I have a strong conviction that the skills of the entrepreneur are invaluable assets for all to have and carry with them throughout their lives, I'm not necessarily saying that everyone should consider traveling the road of entrepreneurship or starting their own small business—though I don't believe that's necessarily a bad idea, depending on each person's situation.

Whether or not you ever have any plans for setting out on your own entrepreneurial journey, I hope you will consider the following reasons I'm going to outline for developing the skills and putting them to work in your own professional life. It is my strong belief that if you do so, you will be far better prepared for whatever path you do choose. The benefits of the entrepreneurial mindset are many—whether you ever work for yourself a day in your life or not.

This mindset cultivates a sense of rugged individualism, yet so much more. It is easy to look around and see example after example of people who put their trust in their career, assuming that it would always exist, yet suddenly found themselves in positions where they had to reinvent their work life.

Sadly, the idea and belief that they could begin anew and acquire whatever new skills might be required of them never seems to cross their mind. It's as though they were programmed (from their past frame of reference and life experiences) that what they had done in the past professionally is what they're meant to do, that it was their identity. Naturally, they end up stuck, and inaction can quickly become as scary as quicksand. Inactivity keeps them from moving ahead.

Contrast the person in this example with a person who has an entrepreneurial mindset and you will notice several key differences. First, they know instinctively that whatever position or job they lost is no more who they were or part of their identity than was their first set of chores they did as a child growing up.

Certainly their past experiences served them, they allowed them to learn an additional skill or skills, but entrepreneurs know firsthand that they can take those skills they've acquired and use them to attract another opportunity into their lives. They also realize that opportunity, though it may not always be in plain view, is always available, and exists for the person who is willing to dig down deep and put the word out that they're looking for it and are open to it should it appear.

It is for this very reason that people with an entrepreneurial mindset will spend time cultivating their network (the people they know personally and professionally) long before they find themselves in need of having to reach out to those folks for help.

One way they develop their network is by ensuring they're always adding more value (doing things that will make others see them as people of value, or a trusted resource) on an ongoing basis. They are careful to avoid being seen as those who only seem to show up when they need something, yet when others need their help, they never seem to be anywhere around.

The person with the entrepreneurial mindset also has a strong sense that even though things and circumstances may change, he or she has within themselves, and with the help of others, the ability to steer things in the right direction.

They avoid at all costs the mentality that tries to convince those without the entrepreneurial mindset that they are somehow dependent solely on circumstances outside of themselves. No, entrepreneurial-minded people approach things such as a job loss as a numbers game. They up the number of people and places they reach out to for new opportunities. They remind themselves of the saying, "You can't always control what happens to you, but you can always control how you react to what happens to you." And they act in accordance with that idea and get on with crafting the life they want as best as they possibly can. Through their actions, they inevitably begin to see the results they are after quickly transpire.

Having this mindset can make you a more valued employee. Some may very well disagree with me here, though I suspect those who do are far more likely to be those same people who haven't studied entrepreneurship nor taken the time themselves to acquire the unique set of skills that comes from doing so. My experience and the first-hand experience I've seen play out through the work I do in the professional development company I own (consulting with clients, and speaking to businesses, large and small), has shown me time and time again that it's true.

CUSTOMER APPRECIATION

One of the unique skills you gain as a result of developing the entrepreneurial mindset is a unique appreciation for and detail to how you interact with and treat customers. If there's one thing all entrepreneurs know—at least if they plan to stay in business for any length of time—is the importance of treating customers as one of your most valuable assets. Without customers, preferably really happy ones who know they're appreciated, one ceases to be in business—and as a result, whether you work for yourself or not, you will cease to have a job. The customer is important—vitally important.

In a small business setting, particularly as you're growing a business, you get to see firsthand just how important retaining your customers is. In the early stages of any business, losing even one customer can be the difference between keeping the lights on or making payroll. When you have that kind of understanding, you will naturally appreciate your customers.

When your customers can see in your actions that they're appreciated, it's possible to create a bond with them so strong that even the monsters of the market-place—the big businesses and corporations that move into your area—can't break. Make no mistake though; forging, keeping, and ever strengthening that special bond between you and your customers is up to you. If you take them for granted during any step of the way, they have the right to move on to a place that will treat them as they deserve to be treated. And make no mistake—that's precisely what they will choose to do.

INCREASING VALUE AS A PROFESSIONAL

An entrepreneurial mindset understands that skills, not entitlements, are what ultimately determine whether one gets ahead or not. Fair or not, the person with the most time in the job isn't always the most qualified or right person to receive advancement in any given job. A person's experience, skill set, and ability to get the job done are more important factors. This statement isn't meant to hurt anyone's feelings, it's just reality. Speaking truth over political correctness is what will serve you, my dear friend—so please accept the truth in what I'm sharing with you, and you will be much better off as a result.

Countless situations have proven that when people have been promoted, in spite of whether or not they were actually the most qualified person for the task, products and people suffered in terms of quality.

With that said, the person with the entrepreneurial mindset actually appreciates the truth in that statement, because he or she knows it's for this very reason they can move more easily up the ladder of success and benefit as a result of it. They know the playing field is truly level; and that their willingness to learn the new skills required of them and apply what they learn going forward will allow them to be in a better-than-average position and to grow within the company. They also know, as mentioned, that if they find themselves in a situation that no longer allows for such growth or professional satisfaction, they can use the skills they've acquired to that point to shift over into a different career field or undertaking.

Whether or not you ever choose to work a day in your life for yourself, having the skills that allow you to do so can and will serve you incredibly well.

The following are action steps for developing the mindset of an entrepreneur. You can try one or all of these ideas. The key is to act on these ideas consistently. Don't make your study of entrepreneurship a one-time event—that's akin to graduating in your career field and never picking up a book or so much as an industry trade journal ever again to keep abreast of the latest happenings. Your skills will stagnate, and your value as a professional will diminish.

- Reach out to entrepreneurs and small business owners in different industries and ask them questions like, "What are the most important skills or attributes you possess as an entrepreneur?"
- Spend time reading books and listening to audio programs that specifically teach entrepreneurial skills and talents.
- A few times a week, preferably daily, visit one of the countless online communities or Websites geared toward entrepreneurs, and read what is being shared and discussed there.
- Work one on one with a coach or mentor who can teach you the skills of the entrepreneur.

Again, those are just a few ideas to get you started. The key difference maker isn't which approach you take, it's that you try one and settle on one that works for you. In doing so, you'll be well on your way to being your best, with a solid set of skills that can serve you, whether or not you use them in the service of another company or make the choice to set out on your own entrepreneurial journey.

A PROUD UNCLE, ENTREPRENEURSHIP, AND NICKEL BOOKMARKS

Upon checking my voice mail one day, I found the most delightful message, "Josh, I had to call, this is your sister. Your youngest nephew came to me earlier this morning and announced that he'd made some bookmarks, and he intended to go out in the neighborhood and sell them. When he told me that, I knew that was a story I had to share with you. I guess he has a bit of his Uncle Josh in him, eh?"

Aside from the fact that I absolutely *adore* my nephews and nieces, I took particular pride in hearing this news. Besides the obvious pride I had for my nephew being bright enough to take the initiative to come up with this idea on his own, I was excited for him because I knew that he'd tapped into something that many, many adults tend to lose sight of over time.

Sadly, as people get older many begin to focus on why things won't work as opposed to simply jumping on the horse and giving themselves a fair shot at the success they deserve…the sense of achievement that is theirs for the taking.

Hearing the story of my nephew reminded me that we're all born with a sense of fearlessness when it comes to pursuing our dreams. I was excited because I knew that his willingness to get out there and do what he wanted to would result in an achievement that will yield results for years to come.

Today it's homemade bookmarks, and who knows, tomorrow it may be a business that he starts that ends up going public. Who is to say for sure, but at just five years old, one thing is for sure—my nephew is off to a good start.

My hope is that you take a moment to reconsider the things that you have put on hold. Ideas that you wanted to pursue, but for whatever reason did not. Do they still hold an appeal for you?

Right now, write those things down. Include a few action steps you can take as quickly as possible to get yourself moving in the right direction. Action in the direction of your desires leads to success, and even the smallest of achievements begins a snowball effect. Keep in mind the saying, "Success begets success."

Another lesson I'd like you to take from the story of my young nephew is that he didn't over plan—something we adults sometimes do too much, often to the point that we end up planning ourselves out of ever taking the action needed to get started. Nope, my little nephew had his idea, made his bookmarks, and before anyone could tell him any differently he headed out the door and got started.

By the way, I'm happy to report that at a nickel a bookmark, he did pretty well.

KEYS FROM STUDYING GREAT ACHIEVERS

I've long been a student of those who have achieved high levels of success. Over the years, I've noticed several common threads in the makeup of the people I've studied. I'd like to recount several of those traits for you in hopes that in identifying them, you can implement the qualities into your life and be better as a result.

Responsibility, Persistence, and Belief in your own greatness. In virtually all the cases I've studied, every person at some point was faced with obstacles that could have kept them from reaching their current level of success. Certainly it would have been easy for each of these individuals to simply blame their life's circumstances for their lot in life and choose to surrender to the idea that greatness was not something they deserved.

Notice I didn't say that the super achievers I've studied did not have issues or pitfalls occur in their lives. No, it's quite the opposite. But what makes them different is that they accepted the shortfalls and went on with the business of overcoming and correcting problems as quickly as possible.

My friend, the fact is that none of us can control where we come from or the poverty that we may or may not have been born into. However, what we can do is begin moving past what stands in our way *now*, and start doing what it takes to improve our place in life now. To accept where you are *now* because you might happen to have less than someone else is not a valid excuse.

I assure you that no matter what might be standing in your way, there is someone in the world who has a story that would put yours or mine to shame. Yet somehow they kept moving forward until they found the key that unlocked what was blocking their way. Just a few examples include Helen Keller, Winston Churchill, Oprah Winfrey, and King George VI—all had to overcome crushing physical and-or emotional limitations.

As you progress on your success journey and begin to believe that you are cut out for greatness, be sure to reach for and review the countless stories of those who have overcome what was in their way and reached their own definition of success. Let these examples be your fuel as you move toward your own dreams.

The reality is that you were born for great things, even if you can't fathom this to be true at this time in your life—I assure you it is still so.

I'm not saying for a moment that it's always going to be an easy path to follow. After all, if life were a bed of roses, we'd all be living the good life. But sadly, that's not so, life takes work, it takes commitment, it takes a lot of persistence, and a commitment to be the best we can possibly be.

If you knew just how much greatness is inside you, I'm convinced it would absolutely amaze you—you would live each day taking more chances because you knew that with each attempt you are one step closer to unlocking greater success.

So my challenge for you at this very moment is to get on with the business of being the best you can be. Dream BIG dreams, plan, and take the action necessary to bring out the great achievements of which you are very capable.

THE IMPORTANCE OF ASKING

Make a point to ask questions. When we simply assume we know the answer to something, there is a chance that we're going to be incorrect. It may very well be that our knowledge or feelings are misguided and that in actuality the other person is simply waiting for us to ask. The reality is that we aren't mind readers—as long as we are careful to ask tactfully, are not pushy, and keep the other person's best interest in mind, then we can ask for answers to questions that they are eager to answer.

Asking is the surest way to get to the answer you're longing to know. One thing is for sure, not asking is certain to get the results you don't want. Ask, you may not always get the answer you hope for, but if you don't ask, you're absolutely certain to get the answer you don't want—which is only going to put you back where you started. Ask, you've got nothing to lose, and everything to gain.

YOUR DREAMS
ARE YOURS FOR THE TAKING

Remember, your dreams are yours for the taking... but...you have to put forth the action it requires to get started as well as keep the faith as you move forward in spite of those who might, intentionally or otherwise, attempt to throw water on your dreams.

You have it in you to live the life you desire. If you didn't, you wouldn't have conceived the idea in the first place. That much I can tell you. Unfortunately what I can't tell you, is the particular mix of perseverance it will take to reach your destination.

So here's a bit of simple advice: Don't give up just shy of your goal, stay in the game even when the chips are down—because very often, you are close to the other side where your goals and dreams reside.

CHECK YOUR COMFORT ZONE AT THE DOOR

No matter what goals and dreams you desire, there's a good chance you will have to reach beyond what you believe yourself to be capable of. This fine line between what you think you can achieve and cannot is often referred to as your comfort zone.

Whether it's giving a report in a class or preparing to make a speech to the board of directors at your company, we all have a point where we begin to doubt what we're made of. Can we really pull it off, we ask ourselves.

Perhaps you're asking yourself something similar at this very moment in your life. Let me assure you—the answer is YES! Yes you can. Now that's not to say you may not be apprehensive or even afraid, or perhaps you can even hear your knees knocking. Fear is simply part of being human, and to some degree, we all deal with it.

The key is to manage fear and not allow it to hold you back. At the risk of belittling something as serious as overcoming your fears, I offer up this acronym for you to keep in mind the next time you find yourself faced with one of life's less-than-comfortable situations:

F = False
E = Evidence
A = Appearing
R = Real

FEAR is actually false evidence appearing real. Keep that saying in mind, and also keep clearly in mind that just beyond your personal comfort zone are great achievements.

GIVE YOUR DREAMS SUBSTANCE

Setting goals is wonderful; it confirms that we've taken those first awkward steps toward attaining what we desire in our lives. The simple fact that you've taken the time to plan what you want to achieve puts you in a distinct class.

Amazingly, few people take the time to keep a running list of goals. Even fewer people actually work toward their goals. So take the time right now to give yourself a little pat on the back if you have written down your goals and dreams. You deserve it!

You are part of the elite group of people who have chosen to take an active role in their own success. If the whole idea of goal setting and goal achieving is new to you, don't worry; the important thing is that you've decided to get started!

Here's a technique to add substance to the goals you've set. Remember, the more real the goal or dream is in your mind, the easier your subconscious mind can get around your desires and jump into action and start helping you realize them!

This technique is offered under the assumption that you've already decided on the things you'd like to achieve. If you're not there yet, then take the time to record your goals, dreams, and the action steps you believe are necessary to reach them. Be sure to give yourself the room to adjust those items as needed. It's a journey and one that you should enjoy. Remember, you're taking the word chance out of the equation and taking an active role in reaching the destinations you set for yourself.

After you've listed your goals and dreams, the next step is to actually visualize yourself reaching your intended goal. Through visualization you can program yourself to reach what you desire.

My friend, it is one thing for you to say, "I want a new job," and quite another to say, "In my dream job I will be in charge of marketing at a growth-oriented company. I will find employment in such and such an industry. To reach this destination I will send out a certain amount of resumes and do follow-ups with those companies until I secure the employment I am looking for."

The idea is that you are rehearsing these events in your mind. You are giving them vast amounts of power because as the saying goes, "That which the mind can conceive, it can achieve." When using visualization with your goals, try to do it as vividly as you can. The more real they appear, the better.

Another technique is to imagine yourself sitting in a movie theater. See your goals and dreams playing out before you on a large screen. Find a technique that works for *you* (the key word being you).

Hopefully from these examples you see the difference that a little visualization can play in making your goals more concrete in your mind. To say you want to find your dream job is one thing, but to identify it and imagine yourself doing this job (and taking the necessary steps to become employed) creates an added energy that will propel you toward making it a reality!

ACTION STEPS

With the following example in mind, write a detailed goal or dream and then visualize it. "My dream is to open a restaurant. I will find people in that industry willing to help me learn about what it takes to run a restaurant. I will contact small business associations, the Chamber of Commerce, and financial institutions to learn about the rules and regulations of the restaurant business. I will follow through with all that I learn and take action to complete necessary paperwork and look for a suitable location."

LIVE BIG:
LET YOUR TALENTS SHINE

"My presence is a gift to this world! It is my duty to live my life to the fullest—not only for my own benefit, but for the many ways that doing so will enhance and make better the lives of everyone around me. Each day I am committed to LIVING BIG!"

LIVE BIG:
WRITE DOWN YOUR ACHIEVEMENT PLAN

"Each day I write down not only what I want to accomplish, but the steps needed to get closer to my intended destination. Even the small steps (so long

as they're steps in the right direction) are moving me ever closer toward where I want to be."

LIVE BIG:
POSITIVE AFFIRMATION:
TRACKING YOUR PROGRESS

"I take the time to evaluate, and where necessary adjust, where I am regarding the goals I have set for myself. In doing so, and in taking action on the items I've identified as most important, I am guaranteed to see progress and move confidently in the direction of what I have determined to be most worthy of attainment. Through persistence, hard work, an honest commitment to action, and a willingness to learn what is needed, I can achieve great things."

LIVE BIG:
ATTRACTING OPPORTUNITIES

"Through ongoing commitment to my own personal and professional development, I am becoming the type of person others seek out and wish to do business with. At the end of each day, I reflect on my progress to make sure I did the little things—those things that show I go above and beyond what's expected. Anyone can do what's expected, but those who are serious about getting ahead look for opportunities to serve others at a greater level. Doing the latter are the things that make me stand out favorably among others in the marketplace. Every day I am moving closer toward the goals I have set. I am as worthy as anyone of achieving success. With each step forward, I am moving confidently in the direction of my dreams and attracting those into my life who can help me get there."

LIVE BIG:
FAN THE FLAMES OF
YOUR DREAMS AND AMBITIONS

"I make a point each and every day to fan the flames of my dreams and ambitions. Each time I look over my written goals and add a little visualization in the form of imagining myself enjoying whatever particular goal I have set for myself, it's like charging the battery that is moving me closer to my heart's desire. I am the only one who can decide whether or not I can achieve what I set out to achieve."

"Poverty, I realized, wasn't only a lack of financial resources; it was isolation from the kind of people that could help you make more of yourself."

–Keith Ferrazzi

Network, ask questions, and learn from successful people as they will help you learn the steps to take in your endeavor to Live BIG!

L E S S O N

15

LEAD THE FIELD

"Productivity is never an accident. It is always the result of a commitment to excellence, intelligent planning, and focused effort."

–Paul J. Meyer

It is important that you study your industry and career field. Having knowledge places you above others who just go to work to put in the time and bring home a paycheck. Strive to be one of the best in your industry.

Whether you work at a manufacturing company, a school, or a high-tech business, those in charge will be impressed if you take the time and initiative to learn as much as possible about the company. It is easy to research companies on the Internet these days, but beware that some sites are not reliable. For instance, Wikipedia's content is not monitored and can be changed by anyone at any time. This is not a credible source. Use instead the company's official Website. Learn the names of those in charge and who are associated with the business. Learn the history and the mission. This knowledge will prove valuable in future conversations.

You may also want to read Websites of your company's competition for insights and opportunities

DEVELOP YOUR SKILLS

Develop the skills necessary that will make you a trusted expert in your given area or endeavor. Many people think they know all there is to know about their job, but there is always something more to learn. Maybe there is a position in another department that has always appealed to you. Maybe your employer has offered you a different position but you turned it down because you were unfamiliar with the tasks.

Now, today, is the time to branch out—to learn more about something, anything that will enhance your resume, your life. As mentioned previously, being a lifelong learner is a key to progressing toward your goals as well as keeping your mind sharp and full of new and exciting people, places, and things.

You may think that you are too old, poor, dumb, or whatever to learn something new, but that is not the case. Have courage! Practice courage by trying. It's less about getting it right all the time, and more about trying your dead-level best, because you will undoubtedly find that as you try your best, it's more than enough to get you to where you want to be.

BALANCE YOUR STRENGTHS
AND AREAS OF IMPROVEMENT

Focus on your strengths. It is easy to look at yourself and see areas that need improvement. While it's true that you should take time for honest reflection on those areas, it's equally important to give yourself due credit for all the wonderful talents you've already acquired—all the bits and pieces that go into making you the incredible person you are.

Please understand that I'm not suggesting we live in lalaland acting as though there's no room for improvements. Of course there are areas in which we all need to improve—that's what personal growth is all about. Instead, what I am suggesting is that we spend at least as much time accepting and being thankful for all the positive traits we have, as on those areas we need to improve.

It's all about balance.

Seek to improve where you can, but be sure to celebrate all that makes up the amazing you as well! Think about it like this, if you want to help someone improve and in the process not have them take it as a personal attack, one way to approach the task would be to compliment them on something they are doing particularly well. Acknowledge and point out one of his or her strengths—making sure it's a genuine and sincere compliment—and then bring up ideas that might be helpful to improve a given area.

Along the same lines, give yourself the same positive boost by acknowledging the good things you're doing, right alongside areas that you've identified where improvement is needed.

Consider the saying, "We become what we think about most." If that statement is even half true, wouldn't it stand to reason that giving a little thought to your past achievements, in addition to any areas in which you'd like to improve, would be a good thing to do? I think so.

Give it a go and see for yourself the positive difference doing so will make.

As for your talents, if you knew how much talent you have inside, I am convinced it would absolutely boggle your mind. The reality is that we all have within us some unique greatness just waiting to find its way into the world. The unfortunate thing is that all too often our talents lay hidden, and we don't always know what they are. Therefore, if we don't take the time to explore and identify our gifts and talents, we run the risk of having them never fully materialize, or lay dormant far longer than they need be.

PRODUCTIVITY—
ALL TASKS ARE NOT CREATED EQUAL

If there's one thing you must grasp to experience an increase in productivity and a strong sense of achievement day to day, it's the concept that not every task is created equal.

This is especially true when it comes to those things that, when completed, will lead to a greater sense of accomplishment and feeling of success and achievement.

Far too many people look at having completed the items on their to do lists as a sure sign that they're achieving at a great level. The problem with this line of thinking is that in many cases the items that make it onto our lists are little more than busy work—items that do require attention, but in the grand scheme of things, having completed them doesn't serve us in a greater capacity with respect to our larger, more important goals. The BIG things that, when completed, actually move us closer to our grand vision, the one we hold for our lives, whether personal or professional, those are the things we need to do.

The challenge is that while you may feel like you are making progress—because after all, you are checking items off during the day—if you are not taking careful inventory and ensuring that the things you are working on will yield your greatest return on investment of time (ROIOT), then it's likely that you will end up feeling as though the larger life plans you hold for yourself aren't making any headway. And this may be correct, not because you aren't working, but because you're not working and putting forth the necessary effort into the specific task needed to yield the exact, true result you are after.

That's why I say, all tasks aren't created equal. Commit this to memory and always be asking the question, "If I work on this task, when completed, will it yield the greatest overall result and sense of accomplishment for me? Will having achieved it move me closer to my larger plan?" If the answer is anything but a resounding Yes! Then you need to reschedule what it is you're planning to work on and replace it with a task that will yield you the greatest ROIOT. It's that simple.

We can decide how to spend our time. We can't, however, decide how much time we have. No matter how hard we try, we can't squeeze any more than twenty four hours out of every day. The good news is that you don't even have to try if you grasp and put into practice the ongoing habit of asking the question just mentioned and working on those items that, when completed, yield the greatest results.

To clarify, I offer a make-believe to do list item, one that might be more in line with busy work, which makes you feel good to finish it, but in the grand scheme of things won't serve you as well as if you instead had chosen to spend your time on other things.

Example To Do item: Vacuum the house.

While this chore is certainly a worthwhile undertaking, is it really as important as your larger goal to increase your sales for the month? No, of course it isn't.

A far more effective use of your time would be to schedule this as a lower priority item, or find a way to have someone else do it for you if possible. While it may feel nice to complete this task, it's not going to yield the same result if you were to replace it with one such as "Place a follow-up call to the people I met at the seminar I attended who showed an interest in my product or service."

As you can see the latter is going to move you closer to what you've identified as your most important goals. Plus, after you've completed the tasks that have the greatest return on your investment of time, then you can go ahead and knock out the other items on the list.

The key thing to remember is that you've got to be vigilant in working on and first completing those items that give you the greatest return on your time spent.

ACHIEVE **BIG** RESULTS
USING SIMPLE SYSTEMS

When I am speaking to groups and organizations, I'll often joke with the audience by telling them I'm the person they bring out when they need something taught in such a simple way that absolutely everyone gets it. Perhaps it is my Southern accent (I'm from Alabama) that often gets the audience chuckling a bit.

I'm only half joking though.

I love simple. Simple works. When things are explained in a simple enough manner, things translate into results. It's in that fashion that I'm going to share what I believe is simple in nature; but if put to work in your daily life, is also quite powerful.

Drum roll please...

I'm talking about developing the habit of creating simple controls to help you accomplish much more in your day-to-day life. Make no mistake, the smaller, seemingly mundane day-to-day tasks all go into determining whether or not you will see through to achievement your larger goals and desired outcomes.

Consider that to accomplish anything worthwhile you will very likely be required to work your way through a given number of smaller things, or as I call them, support tasks. These are things that, while they may be far from glamorous, are nevertheless required to move you closer to your more coveted goal.

For example, to become a great writer, a person has to first begin to write. In many cases, the person doesn't start writing well; often it's the act of doing, that in time, leads to improvement. Getting started and putting pen to paper (or fingers to keyboard) is akin to the support tasks I mentioned.

To further illustrate my point, let's take the following hypothetical situation and then make up and apply some simple systems so we can see firsthand how using them can benefit us.

Let's say I want to develop a positive habit. Nothing monumental necessarily, but rather that I want to take a walk once a day. Notice I didn't say, climb Mount Everest or train for a marathon. We're talking about something I've got the ability to do, something I need to make a conscious, ongoing decision to see it through to the point that it becomes a habit.

For the scenario I suggested, I would use the following simple system:

- Write the words "walk now" or "go for your daily walk," something to that effect in black sharpie marker (it's bolder then regular pen) on several 3x5 index cards.
- I would tape one card on my bedroom door. Why? Because I would be sure to have it staring

me right in the face whenever I went in or out of
the room.

- I would place another card on the dashboard (or
  perhaps attach it right by the radio) of my ve-
  hicle.
- I would place a card on my refrigerator and on the
  desk where my computer is located. Places where
  I'm certain to see the message on each card.
- I would very likely set up a recurring reminder
  on my handy, dandy smart phone.

In short, in a very low-tech way I would bug the tar out
of myself (yes, that's a real saying, I didn't make it up) to
the point where it is just easier to do the thing that needs to
be done.

I'll fully concede that the ideas I just shared with you
are simple in nature. As you can see, the power is in the reminding. Friend, we don't need to know what to do in most
cases, we've already got that part figured out. Rather, we
need only strategically placed reminders in such a way that
we opt to do the activity rather than continue to experience
the ongoing sense of "gentle guilt" that pops up every time
we see one of the cards.

The interesting thing about this approach is that when
you've actually gone for the walk and you see one of the
reminders you've set for yourself, you feel positively about
yourself knowing you followed through. That is, you get
to experience again the positive feelings associated with the
winning feeling of completing your goal, knowing it's moving you that much closer to what you want.

So to sum things up and place a nice BIG blue bow
around what we're talking about here—the simple systems
approach I have shared with you works because there is
great truth in the old saying, "Out of sight, out of mind."

The things we keep front and center tend to get done more often than those things which we lose track of. If this sounds overly simple and repetitious, good. It's supposed to. Remember, I get paid good money to be the guy companies bring out when everyone absolutely must have things explained in such simple terms so that everyone "gets it."

Get creative with the ideas I've shared. Look for ways you can implement your own simple systems to get from "want to", to "finished!" I'd love to hear what you come up with and hope you will share them with me.

ACTION STEP

Visit your company's Website and review any job openings that may be posted. Do any of them look interesting to you? If so, what kind of additional training or skills do you need to acquire? What natural talents can you offer to the position? What areas will you have to improve to fit into that position?

LIVE **BIG**:
CONTINUALLY UPGRADE YOUR SKILLS

"Each day I spend some time investing in myself. The time I put in to improving my skills pays dividends that can never be taken from me. Outside circumstances can change—and though I may find myself with fewer resources through no control of my own, the skills I've developed will always remain. The important thing about this is that even in a worst-case scenario should I have to begin anew, because of the skills I possess I can regain and surpass whatever I may have lost. Therefore, I am diligent in continuously upgrading my skill set."

LIVE **BIG**:
ACQUIRING KNOWLEDGE

"I have the opportunity to excel in whatever endeavor I choose. Through a commitment to ongoing learning and a willingness to apply the acquired knowledge, I have within my grasp the ability to lead the field in whatever I choose to pursue."

LIVE **BIG**:
PRACTICE BEING FEARLESS

"Whenever the opportunity to do so appears (as it often does), I make a point to practice being fearless in my life. Boldness leads to increased opportunity and life's rewards. I may not always get the exact outcome I desire, yet I know that by being courageous and being proactive, I will always give myself a better-than-average chance that positive results will eventually come my way. There is truth in the old saying, 'Fortune favors the brave.' Each day I will do my best to practice being bold—even when it may feel uncomfortable. In doing so, I know that I'm developing a positive habit that will allow me to better reach my full potential."

"You've got to look for a gap, where competitors in a market have grown lazy and lost contact with the readers or the viewers."

–Rupert Murdoch

16

How to Build Win-Win Relationships

"The quality of your life is the quality of your relationships."

–Anthony Robbins

I did it. I added a photo album to my Website. "This," I thought, "I need to do. It will look more professional. It will help people see what I look like—even though that's a bit scary! And, besides, it is fun."

Then came the responses.

After placing the photo album on my Website I immediately received some very positive emails. The positive responses were gratifying and caused me to slow down and reflect about things "on the personal side of life."

In essence, people wrote: "I got to know you a bit better." "You were more than some guy who sent me an email newsletter at the beginning of my day."

Isn't that remarkable? People still value relationships. People still value the personal touch. It is not out of vogue. A few things in life never change, and the value of "the personal side of life" is one of those few things.

Stop and think for a moment. Take yesterday for instance; did you miss any opportunities to add the personal touch to an aspect of your day? What about last week? Last month?

Don't get me wrong: I love technology. After all, that's how I earn my living. But as my friend Bob Burg says: "All things being equal, people will do business with, and refer business to, those people they know, like and trust."

What have you done recently to have someone like you, know you, or trust you?

LIFE IS A JOURNEY, LIVE IT!

Life is quite the adventure. I confess that there are times, where I question my abilities. Incidentally, if you're curious, no, I don't consider that a weakness, instead I call it being human.

Perhaps you can relate to any of the following questions having run through your mind before: Am I as successful as I should be? Have I lived up to my full potential? Should I have done such and such? Should I have chosen this over that? The questions that can pop up are near limitless in scope.

As I mentioned before, questioning isn't a bad thing in itself. It can help keep us on our toes. In fact, in some instances it can help move us from stagnation to a place where we experience just enough uneasiness that we get busy and get on with the business of doing what is required of us to attain whatever we happen to be after.

Questioning becomes a challenge when we find ourselves unable to silence our inner Doubting Thomas and get on with taking whatever action is necessary to move us in the direction we want to go. And make no mistake; movement is a necessity if you want to see greener pastures!

As you move through your day, keep the following saying clearly in mind, *"Life has an amazing way of filling in the details for the person who will practice courage by leaping out in faith and taking action."* Reflect on it, and take notice how it plays out in your life. Let this simple statement lend strength to you when you may be feeling doubt.

If you're stuck in inactivity, no matter how much wishing otherwise you do, you're more than likely going to remain right there where you are — stuck.

On the other hand, if you move even the slightest bit, even if you're not completely sure exactly what steps to take, if you apply some sort of change in direction (inspired action!), you will find more often than not that the very act of doing something was enough to create the necessary forward momentum to get you moving in the right direction.

Friend, you don't have to have all the answers prior to setting out in the pursuit of your goals and dreams. You do have to have the courage to begin — and yes, you will very likely need to move beyond your current comfort zone.

That said, I can promise you that in no time flat you are sure to notice that you have all you need to meet with success, to overcome whatever at first appeared to stand in your way. You will begin to see firsthand that you have countless talents, and God-given gifts. Numerous people, things, and opportunities will begin to appear, and start to transpire, which all work toward moving you toward what you hold to be worthwhile.

Your willingness to take action reveals to you just how capable you are. That perhaps is one of the most interesting things about the achievement process. It's totally possible to remain completely stagnant, if you choose to wait for the right time prior to going for your goals and dreams.

The people who can convince themselves to leap out in seemingly blind faith—giving their best effort—will more often than not find that doing so, in the end, was all that was truly required of them to live a life well worth living, filled with great adventure and a sense of fulfillment.

Don't ask for the journey to be easy or you may well miss it all together. Ask instead for the courage to step out even in your darkest moments; for in doing so, your courage will inevitably be the beacon of light that shines the light on the path necessary to get you to your own definition of success.

As you move forward each day, keep clearly in mind that as long as you continue to move forward in the direction of your dreams, your path will continue to appear, the brush will clear away, and you will attain the place you seek.

Never forget that you were indeed made for greatness. When you show courage through action, you prove that you are worthy of the rich rewards that life holds in store for you.

Do What You Say—An All-Important Key to Getting Ahead

There are any number of things that will either propel you forward, or hold you back when it comes to getting ahead in your professional and personal life. Therefore, it's particularly perplexing for me to witness those people who have an inability to avoid the temptation to make promises or simply tell people what they think they want to hear, then for whatever reason not deliver on what they said.

With the path to greater success often a challenging maze at times, this particular character trait is one that can and should be eliminated. People do not want to do business with, or in many cases be friends with or associate with, those who won't follow through with what they say they will do.

I want to make one very clear distinction about what you just read. I am NOT saying that you have to try to make everyone happy. Even if you tried, you couldn't deliver on everything people ask of you. What I am saying is that if you make an arrangement with someone or tell them you will do something, if you really want to succeed and not have it work against you in the future, you must do your dead-level best to deliver on whatever you agreed to do. Again, there will be times when try as you might, you fall short. In those times admit you did, reach out, and apologize. The next time around, do not repeat the same mistake.

While you may never reach the point where you are able to deliver on 100 percent of the commitments you make (try as you might), you must strive to keep every commitment by not over-reaching yourself or your resources. Integrity in business and in life is a quality to hold tightly, as is respect for those with whom you have relationships—personal and professional.

The thing you must remember, whether intentional or not, the result is often the same—your credibility suffers, and eventually you will garner the reputation as someone who, while you may be a nice person, simply can't be counted on to do what you say. Believe me, it's a label you don't want to wear; and with it being relatively easy to avoid, there's no excuse for you to have to do so.

Going forward, be honest with yourself. If you fall into the trap that I've described, starting now begin to develop habits that will take you from that person to one who at the very least genuinely tries to follow through on what you promise. Whether it's something as simple as returning an email or call that you've committed to, or something far more important like handling part of a sales process, or showing up for a family function, the point is, follow through if you said you would.

Depending on how long this has been part of your character, it may be easier said than done to replace your negative habits with positive ones, but you must stick with it until you do. Not to do so will limit you in ways you simply can't imagine. The people who hold life's great opportunities will steer clear of those who are branded with the label of not doing what they say.

Being aware is one of the most important things you can do to ensure you follow through on what you say you will. The moment that you think about it, you can choose to do what needs to be done—and if you're honest with yourself, you'll admit there's always that moment when you think to yourself about the thing that needs to be done. In the end, you can chose to ignore taking action or take action—that makes the difference.

Keeping simple reminders is another easy way to make sure you follow through on your commitments. If you are truly bogged down to the point that you can't break free and do it yourself, set up a system where someone does it for you, delegate the task; but no matter what, make sure it gets done! Your credibility is simply too important not to take serious.

Again, this isn't coming from someone who makes the claim to never have fallen short myself. Though far more often I've delivered on what I said because I know how important it is. Do your best to follow through.

Over the years, I have seen numerous people who mistakenly believed that making a promise, whether they could actually deliver on it or not, would somehow win them favor. Sadly, in many cases, it not only worked against them, it also left a bad taste in the mouth of the client or customer, for the entire business, even though it was actually just that one person who was at fault. Perhaps worst of all is that in most cases, the promise that was made didn't even have to be committed to at all. The client would have been just as happy either way.

The solution is simple...Make a habit of under-promising and over-delivering. If you can do that, you will find that more often than not you have happy customers; and when it comes to your personal life, you will have an abundance of family and friends who appreciate you, and show it!

Making a promise just because it makes you look good—if you're unable to deliver on it, or even worse, simply have no intention of actually doing so—will mostly likely backfire on you in ways you can't imagine. Don't take that chance—your level of achievement depends on it.

ACTION STEP

Write at least five creative ways you can help people: Like you.

_____

_____

_____

_____

_____

Know you.

_____

_____

_____

_____

_____

Trust you.

_____

_____

_____

_____

_____

LIVE BIG:
THE WORDS YOU USE MATTER

"The language I use, and allow others to use when they refer to me matters. Words have power, they can build folks up, or break people down. While it's true that I can't always control what others say about me, I can control what I accept to be true—and in turn give power to. I can make the choice to tune out what others say when it doesn't help to move me in a positive direction."

LIVE BIG:
THE GOLDEN RULE

"I am always on the lookout to build up others and encourage them to be the best they can possibly be. When I help others unlock their full potential, life will move people into my life who can help me reach my own dreams and goals. I keep clearly in mind the golden rule: Do unto others as you would have them do unto you."

LIVE BIG:
SERVING OTHERS IN A POSITIVE WAY

"Today I will spend time looking for ways to do what is best for others. When I consider the needs of others—and look for ways to genuinely serve them, I create a vacuum effect that may go unseen, but

exists just the same. When I practice acts of kindness, more of that is exactly what makes its way into my own life."

"Relationships of trust depend on our willingness to look not only to our own interests, but also the interests of others."

–Peter Farquharson

Being a trustworthy, sincere, and motivated individual will help you begin the kind of win-win relationships that will lead you to Live BIG!

17

CELEBRATING
SUCCESS

"Celebrate what you want to see more of."
–Thomas J. Peters

It is of great benefit to you to recount the daily achieve-ments you experience. No matter how small or insignifi-cant you may view them at the moment, each should be acknowledged—and framed in your mind—as successes. If you neglect to do so, there's a chance that you will end up focusing on the day's activities that don't help build your self-esteem.

There's great personal power that comes from celebrat-ing both our larger achievements as well as the small suc-cesses that we experience in our lives. The reality is that we have the choice to allow ourselves to gravitate toward thinking about the negative things we have experienced, or we can choose to take a proactive approach to mentally re-live the positive accomplishments of the day.

It really does get right down to making the choice to see things from a half full versus half empty mentality. Make the choice to see the positives—and that's exactly what you'll notice more of during your days.

LIFE IS A NUMBERS GAME—EMBRACE IT!

Friend, doubt stems often from what we believe we are capable of; and since what we see ourselves capable of is often limited by our past experiences or our current frame of reference, it's important that we continually try new things and expand our skill sets beyond where they are now.

Another extremely important lesson I learned very early on was that there's almost always a numbers game component you can apply to certain parts of your life. Here's what I mean: Before I ever picked up the phone to call that first prospective client, I was instructed to look for a "call to prospect ratio." Put simply, this is how many calls, on average, I had to make before a call became a prospect (or in my case, I was able to set an appointment). Interestingly, it didn't take long before certain patterns began to appear.

Equally fascinating to me was that I realized as I got better, as I improved my ability to interact with prospective clients, my call to prospect ratio improved greatly as well. It also showed me firsthand that I had control, at least to some degree, of how well I would do, or could do financially.

One of the things that scares people away from accepting a straight commission type of pay arrangement (or starting a business of their own, or any number of other undertakings in life where the outcome isn't always clear cut), is that they feel as though they have little if any control over their earning potential. While it's largely a manufactured fear in the person's mind, it can appear quite real just the same.

Understanding that I could control my ratio depending on what additional effort I was willing to put in was an essential skill—and one I'm truly thankful to have acquired at such a young age. I can honestly say that this understanding has served me countless times throughout my life, and allowed me to go for opportunities I might have otherwise passed on had I not learned and fully embraced it.

Understanding that you can "play the numbers" in your life has far greater benefits than just the examples I listed. For instance, you can use them to find a relationship after you lost the person you were sure was your soul mate (if at first you don't succeed, try, try, again), stack the deck in your favor in your career search by putting your resume out anywhere you think you would enjoy working, stretching the bounds of what conventional wisdom may say in terms of the "right thing" to do—these are just a few examples of how you can put the ideas to work in your life.

When you understand that you're not a lost ship at sea simply hoping that things will work out, and the wind will magically fill your sails, you begin to realize that you hold the power. Depending on the event or place at which you find yourself, you can choose to stick-it-out just a little while longer, you can change course, or can choose to try something completely different.

The point is—you will suddenly realize that positive things don't usually occur by happenstance. And that you are not meant to sit idle as the winds of life blows you in whichever direction it sees fit. You are an active participant in your own life. The way in which it will play out, the successes and rewards life has to offer you can be yours. You will experience the comfort that comes from knowing that your actions do make a difference.

ACKNOWLEDGE YOUR ACCOMPLISHMENTS

Are you patting yourself on the back enough? Chances are if you're moving too hastily toward your intended goals, you're not taking ample time to enjoy your accomplishments. There are many benefits to taking the time to acknowledge your accomplishments.

When you take due credit for a job well done, it helps to crystallize in your mind that you are making progress. This in and of itself is reason enough to "stop and smell the roses," as the saying goes. Not to mention that acknowledging how far you have come so far helps recharge your internal batteries, which gives you the get up and go you need to make things happen in your life!

Simply put, take pleasure in your efforts! Doing so helps remind you that what you are doing is worth the effort. Here's hoping you are well on your way to your own definition of personal success. Incidentally, if you still aren't clear about what success means to you, take a little time to define it. It's hard to hit a target when you don't really know what it is.

ACTION STEP

At the end of each day just before falling off to sleep, take a moment to write down several successes from the day. Remember that they don't have to be monumental to count as a success. Anything from meeting a new person, calling on a new client, showing kindness to someone, or anything in between qualifies as a worthy achievement. After you have written the list, read each of the items, and each time close your eyes for a moment and try to experience the positive feelings associated with that given accomplishment.

LIVE BIG:
BEING DILIGENT

"The difference is in the details. I take comfort in knowing that I don't have to get every single thing right, nor do I have to make every correct choice on the path toward achieving my goals (after all, each misstep, when corrected and learned from can be a valuable teacher). Instead, so long as I stay plugged into and working diligently on those tasks necessary to reach my intended destination, I will experience success."

LIVE BIG:
FOCUS ON WHAT YOU CAN CONTROL

"I make a point to stay plugged in to the things I can control. When I focus on what I can control, rather than the things I cannot, I am putting myself in a position to accomplish the goals I've set for myself. The sense of achievement I long for is found in doing the best I can in the things I can control, and limiting the amount of time I allow myself to get caught up in the things I can't."

LIVE BIG:
CONSISTENT ACTION

"I am moving ever forward toward the goals I have set for myself. I take comfort in knowing that I don't have to knock the ball out of the park every day to reach the level of success I desire. I need only stay plugged into and work diligently on the tasks required of me, and eventually I am

guaranteed to reap the rewards life has to offer for doing so."

> "For the rational, psychologically healthy man, the desire for pleasure is the desire to celebrate his control over reality."
>
> –Nathaniel Branden

For future success, celebrate all the ways you have chosen to Live BIG!

EPILOGUE

"Life is too short to be little."

—Benjamin Disraeli

Friend, I hope you have enjoyed what I have shared with you.

I want to make one thing clear; the point is not for you to fully grasp everything covered in the lessons above right out of the gate. In fact, it is likely that you will come to fully appreciate the wisdom shared over time, as you begin to implement the ideas and see for yourself the positive impact doing so has on you, both personally and professionally.

One more thing you must understand, at this point, as we come to the end of our time together, you may find yourself at a bit of a crossroad. Down one road, you can opt to never come back or put into practice the many ideas and life strategies that you have just learned. That, friend, is one choice. The choice to do absolutely nothing, other than file away the ideas you learned into some deep place in your mind would be a terribly unwise decision.

Should you decide to take the other road, it can lead to a life filled with wonder and untold achievements that you can't now fully fathom in your wildest dreams. Countless people before you over many generations have used a number of the techniques and strategies you have just been given to craft their own best lives.

Friend, you have the tools and knowledge, but make no mistake, knowledge itself is not enough, what will be the true difference is your ability to apply what you have learned in a consistent, persistent manner.

Do that, and your life can truly be whatever you wish it to be.

It's your life, LIVE BIG!

Josh Hinds

About the Author

Josh Hinds is a proven mentor, inspirational speaker, and entrepreneur. He started his first online business in 1996, an online community for those interested in personal and professional development. In addition to his growing network of professional development websites, Josh is the founder of GetMotivation.com an empowering and inspiring community website which has been visited by millions.

You can visit Josh, and learn more about the work he does at www.JoshHinds.com.